Monday Nights in NAUVOO

JANET BURNINGHAM

To Katey and Maddy

Monday Nights in NAUVOO

Lessons and Games for Family Home Evening
Based on the Doctrine and Covenants
and Church History

JANET BURNINGHAM

CFI
Springville, Utah

ISBN 978-1-59955-206-4

Published by CFI, an imprint of Cedar Fort, Inc., 2373 W. 700 S., Springville, UT, 84663
Distributed by Cedar Fort, Inc. www.cedarfort.com

LIBRARY OF CONGRESS CATALOGING-IN-PUBLICATION DATA

Burningham, Janet.
Monday nights in Nauvoo : lessons, stories, and games for family home evening : from the doctrine and covenants / Janet Burningham.
p. cm.
ISBN 978-1-59955-206-4
1. Family home evenings (Mormon Church) 2. Doctrine and Covenants--Criticism, interpretation, etc. I. Title.

BX8643.F3B88 2008
249--dc22

2008025348

Cover design by Nicole Williams
Edited and typeset by Jessica Stout

Printed in the United States of America

10 9 8 7 6 5 4 3 2 1

Printed on acid-free paper

Contents

APPENDIX

Acknowledgments

I would like to thank my children for the time they eagerly spent reading through these lessons and answering numerous questions. Your love of the scriptures and your desire to learn is my inspiration and motivation; without you these books would not be written.

I especially want to thank my husband, Scott, for believing in me and cheering me on. Your faith in me keeps me going.

Thank you to all my friends and family for supporting me and encouraging me to take what was initially written for just my family and to give it to others.

Thank you to my nephew Spencer Wood for the brilliant illustrations that add so much to this book. The giving of your talents so willingly is much appreciated.

An extra big thank you goes to Cedar Fort, Inc. for taking a chance on me and for making my dream a reality. The editors and staff are some of the nicest people I have ever worked with.

And finally, I offer my deepest gratitude to my Heavenly Father. Thank you for loving me, teaching me, and inspiring me. Everything good that I do and have comes through You.

Introduction

Now, more than ever, our children need to have testimonies of the gospel at a young age. Family home evening and family scripture study are essential to making this happen. Children's faith and courage will be strengthened as they study the words of the Lord and learn to apply His teachings in their lives.

However, studying from the scriptures is not always easy with children—especially the Doctrine and Covenants, since it doesn't have stories like the Book of Mormon.

The lessons in this book are simple, engaging, and effective. They were designed to help transition children from picture scriptures to the actual scriptures, and to help build knowledge and comprehension of important gospel principles taught in the Doctrine and Covenants.

I know from experience that regular scripture study can be challenging. However, setting up a schedule and only reading the amount of verses that are age appropriate for your family is important in making it a memorable, uplifting experience.

The blessings that come into your home from studying the scriptures together are immeasurable and priceless. The scriptures will draw your family closer to our Father in Heaven and His Son, Jesus Christ. A spirit of love and kindness will be felt, and families will grow closer together. I bear testimony that this is true and pray for the Lord's spirit and blessings to be with your family as you begin a study of the Doctrine and Covenants.

How to Use This Book

Hi! My name is Simeon, and I am a scripture guide. You might remember me from *Monday Nights in Zarahemla* where I helped guide you through the Book of Mormon. I'm excited to be with you now as you journey through the Doctrine and Covenants, and discover important truths and lessons. Joseph Smith and the early members of The Church of Jesus Christ of Latter-day Saints were faithful, courageous people and you can learn a lot by studying about them!

There are both lessons and stories in this book; the stories do not contain verses from the Doctrine and Covenants but are included to help you understand important events that were happening at that time in the Church. Each story includes questions and can be studied separately from the lessons.

In each of the lessons, you will find:

BACKGROUND INFORMATION

Before beginning each lesson, make sure you read the background. Many of the sections in the Doctrine and Covenants were received because of people or things that were happening in the Church at that time. To better understand each section, it is important to know the events preceding the revelation.

GOSPEL ART PICTURE KIT

This references which picture from the Church's gospel art picture kit would correspond with the lesson. You can hold or display a picture while studying the lesson. The back of each picture includes information that might be helpful to read prior to studying the lesson.

WORD QUEST

Learning the language of the scriptures is very important in being able to understand them. At the top of each lesson you will find a list of words. You might want to assign a word or two to each person in your family before you begin. Each person is responsible for looking for their word while you are reading. When you get to each word, stop and talk about the meaning. Easy-to-understand definitions for each word are given in the lesson. There's also a glossary in the back of the book where you can keep track of the new words and their definitions.

VERSES

The Doctrine and Covenants is filled with gospel principles that are important for children to know but are not always easy to understand. Therefore, only the sections and verses that pertain to significant Church history events or to most children's lives are included in this guide. Parents are encouraged to read additional sections and verses that they feel their family would benefit from.

SUGGESTED QUESTIONS

A series of simple comprehension and application questions are provided with each section of verses.

There are several ways in which the verses and questions can be studied. (1) Read the questions before reading the verses. Some children (especially younger children) may benefit from having the questions given to them before they read a particular verse. This gives them something to look for while they are reading, and helps them better understand the verse. (2) Read each section of verses like it is shown. Then stop to read the corresponding questions. This helps ensure that children comprehend what they are reading. (3) Read through all the verses listed and then go back and read the questions. Older children might prefer this approach. (Note: The verses in which the answers can be found are given in parentheses next to the questions.)

TREASURES OF KNOWLEDGE

Included in each lesson are explanations that may further enhance your understanding of the scriptural passages you have read. Parents are encouraged to read these explanations and talk about them with their children; important discussions will often take place when teaching these gospel truths to your children. The definitions for the words listed in the Word Quest are also found here.

In the appendix you will find several study aids that can be helpful in better understanding the Doctrine and Covenants.

CHURCH HISTORY TIMELINE

This timeline provides a quick overview of the major Church history events that are studied in this guide.

CHURCH HISTORY MAP

Use this map when you are studying the lessons related to the different areas where the Saints lived.

WHO'S WHO IN THE DOCTRINE AND COVENANTS

This section is a list and description of the people in the Doctrine and Covenants. It includes where and when they lived, along with a brief synopsis of their lives.

WORD QUEST GLOSSARY

This list includes all the words from each "Word Quest." No definitions are given here. This is where children can write down the definitions as they learn them, which will help them to remember the definitions better.

GAMES, GAMES, GAMES!

This section is a list and description of the people in the Doctrine and Covenants who are mentioned in the lessons. Most games can be adapted to fit both older and younger children.

SCRIPTURE STRIPS

A great way to mix things up and have some fun! Cut out the titles listed and place them in a container. Each time your family gathers for family home evening or scripture study, let someone choose which story or lesson to study by picking a title from the container.

What Is the Doctrine and Covenants?

The Doctrine and Covenants contains revelations given by the Lord Jesus Christ to His prophets in the Latter-days. Just as the Lord gave revelations to prophets in Old Testament times, New Testament times, and Book of Mormon times, He still speaks to His prophets today.

Joseph Smith, the first prophet in this dispensation, received many important revelations from the Lord regarding His will for His Church and its members.

In 1830, Church members were desirous to obtain copies of the revelations Joseph had received, so at a conference it was decided to copy and print the revelations. After the conference Joseph prayed to know if doing so was the Lord's will. In answer to his prayer, Joseph received the revelation that is now Doctrine and Covenants section one.

This section is often referred to as the Lord's Preface, which is why it was placed at the beginning of the book. In this revelation the Lord gives His approval for the printing of the revelations:

> Behold, this is mine authority, and the authority of my servants, and my preface unto the book of my commandments, which I have given them to publish unto you, O inhabitants of the earth…
>
> Behold, I am God and have spoken it; these commandments are of me, and were given unto my servants in their weakness, after the manner of their language, that they might come to understanding…
>
> Search these commandments, for they are true and faithful, and the prophecies and promises which are in them shall all be fulfilled. (D&C 1:6, 24, 37)

In September 1831, W. W. Phelps purchased a printing press at the request of Joseph Smith, and by November 1831 leaders of the Church decided to publish three thousand copies of the revelations and call it the *Book of Commandments*. However, in July 1833, a mob attacked W. W. Phelps's home and printing press, and most of the copies he had printed were destroyed. This delayed the publication of the revelations until 1835, when the revelations, now titled *Doctrine and Covenants* were printed, bound, and available for purchase. This edition contained 102 revelations and a section titled *Lectures on Faith*; seven lectures given by Joseph Smith to the School of the Prophets in Kirtland, Ohio.

In 1844, an edition containing 111 sections was printed, and by 1876 there were 136 sections. In 1921, Elder James E. Talmage of the Quorum of the Twelve Apostles was assigned to write the headings for each section, make some format changes, and add an index. *Lectures on Faith* were removed at this time because they were not considered official revelations.

Our current edition of the Doctrine and Covenants was last edited in 1981, where two more sections, two official declarations, new footnotes, new section headings, and historical information was added.

President Joseph Fielding Smith emphasized the importance of the Doctrine and Covenants to Church members today. He stated that "It is our book. It belongs to the Latter-day Saints.… If we value it, understand it, and know what it contains, we will value it more than wealth; it is worth more to us than the riches of the earth."*

Optional: Read and discuss the Explanatory Introduction found at the beginning of the Doctrine and Covenants.

* *Doctrine and Covenants Student Manual* (Salt Lake City: The Church of Jesus Christ of Latter-day Saints, 2001), 2.

LESSON ONE

Joseph Smith

BACKGROUND

Joseph Smith was the first prophet of The Church of Jesus Christ of Latter-day Saints. Most of the revelations in the Doctrine and Covenants were given to Joseph Smith by Jesus Christ. In 1838, when Joseph was thirty-five years old, he wrote a history of his life and of the Church. Part of that history is included in the Pearl of Great Price in our scriptures; it is called Joseph Smith—History (JS—H).

GOSPEL ART PICTURE KIT

401

WORD QUEST
- sect
- proselyte
- poignant
- aloof
- denominations

VERSES	SUGGESTED QUESTIONS	TREASURES OF KNOWLEDGE
JS—H 1:3–5	• When and where was Joseph Smith born? (v. 3) • What was Joseph's father's name? (v. 3) • What were the names of Joseph's mother, brothers, and sisters? (v. 4) • Explain what the "unusual excitement" was about. (v. 5) • What do you think the people of the different religions were arguing about?	**sect:** a church with a particular belief Did you know that Joseph from the Bible ("Joseph and the coat of many colors") prophesied that Joseph Smith would have the same first name as him, and that Joseph Smith's father's name would also be Joseph? (See 2 Nephi 3:15)
JS—H 1:7–8	• How old was Joseph at this time? (v. 7) • Which members of his family joined the Presbyterian faith? (v. 7) • Why do you think Joseph thought seriously about which church to join? (v. 8) • Which church was Joseph considering joining? (v. 8) • Describe some of the feelings Joseph had when deciding which church to join. (v. 8)	**proselyte:** to persuade someone to convert to one's faith **poignant:** intense, heartfelt **aloof:** distant **denominations:** religious groups

LESSON TWO

The First Vision

BACKGROUND

Read lesson "Joseph Smith" prior to this lesson.

GOSPEL ART PICTURE KIT

402, 403

WORD QUEST

- tumult
- liberally
- upbraideth
- venture
- amidst
- exerting
- defy
- creeds
- abomination
- forbade
- adversary

VERSES	SUGGESTED QUESTIONS	TREASURES OF KNOWLEDGE
JS—H 1:10–12	• What questions did Joseph ask himself? (v. 10) What verse of scripture did Joseph read, and what did it say? (v. 11) • What does the verse in James 1:5 mean, and who does it apply to? • What were Joseph's feelings about the scripture he read? (v. 12)	**tumult:** confusion **liberally:** generously **upbraideth:** to criticize (God will not be angry with you for asking Him questions)
JS—H 1:13–14	• What did Joseph decide he needed to do? (v. 13) • Where and when did Joseph go to pray to God? (v. 14) • Was this the first time Joseph had prayed out loud? (v. 14)	**venture:** to try, even when the outcome is uncertain **amidst:** surrounded by
JS—H 1:15–17	• What happened after Joseph began to pray, and how do you think he felt? (v. 15) • Who was trying to stop Joseph from praying and why? (v. 16) • Describe what Joseph saw over his head. (v. 16) • How was Joseph delivered from Satan? (v. 17) • What can we learn from Joseph's example about what to do when Satan tempts us? • Describe who Joseph saw in the light. (v. 17) • What did Heavenly Father say to Joseph? (v. 17)	**exerting:** using **defy:** challenge (there are no words that can describe the heavenly vision Joseph saw)

VERSES	SUGGESTED QUESTIONS	TREASURES OF KNOWLEDGE
JS—H 1:18–20 * Gordon B. Hinckley, "The Stone Cut Out of the Mountain," *Ensign*, November 2007, 83. ** Hoyt W. Brewster Jr., *Doctrine and Covenants Encyclopedia* (Salt Lake City: Deseret Book, 1988), 3.	• What did Joseph ask Heavenly Father and Jesus, and what was their answer? (vv. 18–19) • What did Jesus tell Joseph about the other churches? (v. 19) • What did Jesus forbid Joseph to do? (v. 20) • How did Joseph feel after the light departed? (v. 20) • What did Joseph tell his mother? (v. 20) • Why did Satan want to stop Joseph? (v. 20) • Why do you think the First Vision was so important and what revealed truths are you most grateful to know? • Discuss why it is important to find out for ourselves if Joseph Smith really did see Heavenly Father and Jesus, if he is a true prophet, of the importance of gaining a testimony of the First Vision. • President Gordon B. Hinckley said: "You and I are faced with the stark question of accepting the truth of the First Vision and that which followed it. On the question of its reality lies the very validity of this Church. If it is the truth, and I testify that it is, then the work in which we are engaged is the most important work on the earth."* • Challenge each family member to read the story of the First Vision alone, to pray about it, and to ask Heavenly Father if it is true.	**creeds:** beliefs **abomination**: "an object, practice, or teaching that is disgusting, detestable, and offensive"** **forbade (forbid):** to command someone not to do something **adversary:** one who opposes or is against, such as Satan and his followers. Isaiah, a prophet from the Old Testament, prophesied about what Jesus said to Joseph in the Sacred Grove (see Isaiah 29:12–13, 2 Nephi 27:24–25, and JS—H 1:19). "Draw near to me with their lips, but their hearts are far from me" means that someone says he believes in Christ, but he doesn't act like Christ does. After Jesus and His apostles died, the priesthood power and many truths were lost. Many churches believed God the Father, Jesus Christ, and the Holy Ghost were one Being, and many believed they were only spirits. The First Vision answered the question of the nature of the Godhead. God the Father and His Son, Jesus Christ, are separate beings with bodies of flesh and bone.

LESSON THREE

The Angel Moroni

BACKGROUND

After Joseph received the First Vision, he told a preacher about it. The preacher was upset by Joseph's story, and even told Joseph that his vision was from the devil. Many people did not believe Joseph and were mean to him and his family. Even though Joseph was treated very badly, he never denied his vision (see JS—H 1:21–25).

Three years later, Joseph prayed to the "Almighty God for forgiveness of all (his) sins and follies, and also for a manifestation to (him), that (he) might know of (his) state and standing before him; for (he) had full confidence in obtaining a divine manifestation, as (he) previously had one" (JS—H 1:29).

GOSPEL ART PICTURE KIT

404

WORD QUEST

- bosom
- countenance
- kindreds
- tongues
- seer
- conduit
- ascended
- musing
- forbidden

VERSES	SUGGESTED QUESTIONS	TREASURES OF KNOWLEDGE
JS—H 1:30–32	• What happened while Joseph was praying? (v. 30) • Describe the personage Joseph saw. (vv. 31–32) • Was Joseph afraid when he saw the angel? (v. 32)	**bosom:** chest **countenance:** the appearance of a person's face
JS—H 1:33–35	• Who was the personage? (v. 33) • Name four things Moroni told Joseph. (vv. 33–34) • Describe the Urim and Thummin and explain its purpose. (v. 35) • How do you think Moroni's prophesy that Joseph's name "should be both good and evil spoken of among all people" has been fulfilled?	**kindreds:** the people of the earth **tongues:** languages **seer:** "a revelator and a prophet" (see Mosiah 8:15–17) Fulness of the everlasting gospel "does not mean it contains every teaching, or every doctrine ever revealed. Rather, it means … we will find the fulness of those doctrines required for our salvation. And they are taught plainly and simply so that even children can learn the ways of salvation and exaltation."*

* Ezra Taft Benson, "The Book of Mormon—Keystone of Our Religion," *Ensign*, November 1986, 4.

Note: Verses 37–39 and D&C 2 contain the words that Moroni gave to Joseph Smith that night. They will be studied at the end of the lesson.

VERSES	SUGGESTED QUESTIONS	TREASURES OF KNOWLEDGE
JS—H 1:42–43	• What did Moroni tell Joseph not to do? (v. 42) • How did Joseph know where to find the hidden plates? (v. 42) • Describe what the room looked like when Moroni left it. (v. 43)	**conduit:** a passage **ascended:** to travel up **musing:** thinking deeply Moroni appeared two more times to Joseph that night and repeated the same message. The next day while Joseph was out working, Moroni appeared again and repeated the same message. Afterwards Joseph walked to the hill where the plates were hidden.
JS—H 1:51–52	• Describe the hill where the plates were hidden. (v. 51) • Was Joseph able to locate the plates? (v. 52) • What else was buried with the plates? (v. 52) • Describe the box that the plates were buried in. (v. 52)	

Note: Moroni warned Joseph the night before that Satan would tempt Joseph to take the plates for money to help his poor family. On the way to the hill Moroni's prophesy came true, for Joseph felt "within him the striving of two invisible powers … the evil one presented alluring prospects of worldly gain from the possession of the plates of gold [or] the better influence whispered that the record was sacred and must only be used for the glory of God and the fulfillment of His purposes."*

* George Q. Cannon. *Life of Joseph Smith the Prophet* (American Fork, UT: Covenant Communications, 2007), 28.

VERSES	SUGGESTED QUESTIONS	TREASURES OF KNOWLEDGE
JS—H 1:53–54	• What happened when Joseph tried to take the plates out? (v. 53) • Why do you think Joseph was not able to have the plates at this time? • How many years would pass until Joseph could get the plates? (v. 53) • What did Joseph do every year for the next four years, and what did he learn each year? (v. 54)	**forbidden:** commanded against, not allowed
Optional: JS—H 1:36–39 or D&C 2	• The prophet Elijah will return before what event? (JS—H 1:38 or D&C 2:1) • What will Elijah plant in the hearts of the children? (JS—H 1:39 or D&C 2:2) • Where will the children's hearts turn? (JS—H 1:39 or D&C 2:2) • What will happen if the prophesy given by Moroni is not fulfilled? (JS—H 1:39 or D&C 2:3)	Elijah was the last Old Testament prophet to hold the sealing powers (see Bible Dictionary, "Elijah," 664). "The great and dreadful day of the Lord" is a reference to the Second Coming of Jesus Christ to the earth. It will be a great day for the righteous. However it will be a dreadful day of judgment and wrath for the wicked. Sealing powers come from God. This means the priesthood ordinances such as baptism, temple marriage, and priesthood ordinations that are performed on earth will still be with us when we die. Without the sealing powers being revealed by Elijah, the earth could not receive celestial glory. "The absence of such powers would result in an earth being barren of eternal family units and thus void of purpose. Hence, man's mortal experience and the earth's purpose would be wasted."*

* L. G. Otten and C. M. Caldwell. *Sacred Truths of the Doctrine and Covenants* (Springville, UT: LEMB, Inc., 1982), 17.

LESSON FOUR
The Gold Plates

GOSPEL ART PICTURE KIT

405, 406

STORY

On September 21, 1823, Joseph was visited by the angel Moroni and told about the gold plates hidden in the Hill Cumorah. Joseph was not allowed to take the plates at that time, but was told to come back to the hill every year for four years to receive instruction.

During this four-year period, Joseph moved to the state of Pennsylvania to work and live. While living with the Hale family, he met and married Emma Hale in January 1827. However, because of rumors and persecution, Emma's family was against the marriage, so Joseph and Emma moved back to New York to live with Joseph's family.

In September 1827, after four years of being taught from the angel Moroni, Joseph was finally entrusted with the gold plates.

Joseph described the gold plates as being six inches by eight inches in size, about six inches thick, and part of it was sealed. The pages, said Joseph, "were filled with engravings, in Egyptian characters, and bound together

in a volume as the leaves of a book, with three rings running through the whole."*

When Joseph received the gold plates, he was told that he could show them to no one, not even his wife and family. He was also warned there would be people who would try and steal them. According to Joseph,

> I soon found out the reason why I had received such strict charges to keep them safe, and why it was that the messenger had said that when I had done what was required at my hand, he would call for them. For no sooner was it known that I had them, than the most strenuous exertions were used to get them from me. Every stratagem that could be invented was resorted to for that purpose. The persecution became more bitter and severe than before, and multitudes were on the alert continually to get them from me if possible. But by the wisdom of God, they remained safe in my hands, until I had accomplished by them what was required at my hand. (JS—H 1:60)

Because of the intense persecution, Joseph and Emma moved back to Pennsylvania where Joseph began to translate what was written on the gold plates by means of the Urim and Thummin. Joseph met a man named Martin Harris who helped the Smiths by giving them money. He also helped Joseph in the translation work of the gold plates.

Martin's wife, Lucy, did not believe Joseph was telling the truth about the plates, and was upset that her husband was spending so much time and money on Joseph. Even though Lucy Harris had been given a dream where she was shown the plates, she was still unconvinced of their existence and was very critical of Joseph.**

After completing 116 pages of translation work from the Book of Lehi, Martin asked Joseph if he could take the manuscript pages home to show his wife. Joseph prayed about it, and the Lord told him not to let Martin take the manuscript. But Martin kept asking, so Joseph prayed again. After the third time, the Lord told Joseph that Martin could take the manuscript, but he could only show it to certain people. Martin broke his promise and the pages were lost.

Joseph was extremely upset by the loss of the manuscript, and felt he had let the Lord down. For a short period of time the plates and the Urim and Thummin were taken away from Joseph by the angel Moroni, but Moroni returned the Urim and Thummin so Joseph could receive the revelation recorded in D&C 3. Afterwards Moroni took them back until Joseph showed sincere repentance. Both the Urim and Thummin and the plates were later returned, and Joseph was allowed to translate again. D&C 10 is the Lord's instructions

* Joseph Smith. *History of The Church of Jesus Christ of Latter-day Saints.* Edited by B. H. Roberts. 2d ed. rev. 7 vols. (Salt Lake City: The Church of Jesus Christ of Latter-day Saints, 1932–51), 4:537.

** *Church History in the Fulness of Times* (Salt Lake City: The Church of Jesus Christ of Latter-day Saints, 2000), 47.

to Joseph on the lost pages and his translation of the gold plates.

SUGGESTED QUESTIONS

- What was the name of Joseph's wife, and when were they married?
- When was Joseph allowed to have the gold plates?
- Describe the gold plates.
- What happened when people found out that Joseph had the gold plates?
- Why didn't Joseph just show them to people instead of hiding them?
- How did Martin Harris help Joseph and Emma?
- Why did Martin want to show the manuscript to his wife?
- What did the Lord tell Joseph when he first asked if Martin could take the manuscript?
- How many times did Joseph ask the Lord if Martin could take the manuscript, and what did the Lord finally say?
- What happened to the manuscript, and what was Joseph's response?
- What happened to the gold plates and the Urim and Thummin after the pages were lost?
- What does this story teach you about accepting the Lord's answers to our prayers?
- What other lessons did you learn from this story?

LESSON FIVE

The Lost Manuscript

BACKGROUND

Read the story "The Gold Plates" before this lesson.

WORD QUEST

- cunning
- suffer
- confound
- abridgement

VERSES	SUGGESTED QUESTIONS	TREASURES OF KNOWLEDGE
D&C 10:1–3	• Where did Joseph get the power to translate? (v. 1) • What happened to Joseph after the pages were lost? (v. 2) • Did Joseph get the gift of translation back? (v. 3) • What did the Lord counsel Joseph to do? (v. 3)	See JS—H 1:35 for an explanation of the Urim and Thummin. After finding out about the lost manuscript, Joseph cried out, "'All is lost! all is lost! What shall I do? I have sinned—it is I who tempted the wrath of God…' He wept and groaned, and walked the floor continually."*
D&C 10:8–11	• Who took the manuscript pages? (v. 8) • What did Satan plan to do with the lost pages? (v. 10, 11)	
D&C 10:12–14	• What did the devil want to do? (vv. 12–13) • What would the Lord not allow? (v. 14) • How do you think the Lord knew what Satan's plan was? • How does it make you feel to know that God knows what Satan's plans are, even long before Satan does them?	**cunning:** hiding the real purpose of someone's plans **suffer:** allow
D&C 10:30, 38	Did the Lord want Joseph to retranslate the book of Lehi (v. 30)? • Where was there another account given of the things Joseph had written on the 116 pages? (v. 38)	

* *Church History in the Fulness of Times* (Salt Lake City: The Church of Jesus Christ of Latter-day Saints, 2000), 48.

VERSES	SUGGESTED QUESTIONS	TREASURES OF KNOWLEDGE
D&C 10:41–43	• What parts of the book of Nephi did the Lord want Joseph to translate? (v. 41) • By not allowing Satan to destroy His work, what does the Lord teach us about His wisdom?	**confound:** to confuse
D&C 10:44–45	• What part of the translation did the wicked men have? (v. 44) • What was engraved upon the plates of Nephi? (v. 45) • For how long had the Lord been preparing for the coming forth of the Book of Mormon? And why do you think the Book of Mormon is so important?	**abridgement:** a shorter version When Nephi was writing his history (over two thousand years before), the Lord knew that the 116 pages of the Book of Lehi would be lost. So the Lord told Nephi to include a history of his family in his own writings that was similar to his father Lehi's history. The Lord also inspired Mormon when he was compiling the Book of Mormon, to add the plates of Nephi to the gold plates. (See 1 Nephi 9:2–6 and Words of Mormon 1:3–7.)

LESSON SIX

Personal Revelation

BACKGROUND

Oliver Cowdery was a school teacher who lived in the same area as Joseph Smith's family. He had heard about Joseph's vision and about the gold plates. Oliver prayed about the things he had heard and received an answer that they were true.

Oliver decided he wanted to meet Joseph. Joseph was living in Pennsylvania at the time and was in need of a scribe (since Martin Harris was no longer allowed to help). A few days after arriving in Pennsylvania, Oliver began to help Joseph in the translation of the gold plates.

After a short time, Oliver wanted to know if he could also translate from the plates, so Joseph asked the Lord and was told that Oliver could attempt to translate. However, Oliver, who was much more educated than Joseph, was unable to translate from the gold plates.

In the following revelations that Joseph received for Oliver, the Lord teaches Oliver (and us) how to ask for and receive personal revelation.

GOSPEL ART PICTURE KIT

416

WORD QUEST

- Zion
- save
- enlighten
- verily
- trifle

VERSES	SUGGESTED QUESTIONS	TREASURES OF KNOWLEDGE
D&C 6:5–7	• What do you think the phrase "If you knock it shall be opened" means? • What two things does the Lord expect us to do when we are asking for help? (v. 6) • What should we want more than being rich? (v. 7) • Why do you think knowing God is a greater blessing than being rich?	**Zion:** Zion is often referred to as both a physical location and a state of the heart. "And the Lord called his people Zion, because they were of one heart and one mind, and dwelt in righteousness; and there was no poor among them" (Moses 7:18). A Zion society follows the same laws as those in the celestial kingdom.
D&C 6:15–16	• What is one way God will answer our questions? (v. 15) • Besides ourselves, who else knows our thoughts and intents? (v. 16)	**save:** except **enlighten:** to give spiritual knowledge "Enlightened by the spirit of truth" means to be taught truths by the Holy Ghost. Ideas and thoughts will come to your mind, and you will know and understand things that you didn't before.
D&C 6:22–24	• What did Oliver pray to the Lord about? (v. 22) • In what way did God answer Oliver? (v. 23) • Review the steps individuals need to take when seeking the Lord's guidance (see D&C 9:8–9, "Treasures of Knowledge"). • Remind family members to follow these steps the next time they make a decision in which they need the Lord's help.	God's witness of the truth often comes with a feeling of peace in our mind and hearts. Elder Richard G. Scott taught that "the feeling of peace is the most common confirming witness that I personally experience."*

* *Church History in the Fulness of Times* (Salt Lake City: The Church of Jesus Christ of Latter-day Saints, 2000), 48.

VERSES	SUGGESTED QUESTIONS	TREASURES OF KNOWLEDGE
D&C 8:1–2	• What three things do we need to have when we ask, in order to receive knowledge? (v. 1) • What do you think it means to have an honest heart when we pray? • The Lord's answers will come to our ____ and our ____, and by _____ (v. 2)	**verily:** in truth, certainly Someone who prays with a desire to know the truth is sincere; they truly want God's help and wisdom. When the Holy Ghost dwells in your heart you will feel comforted and at peace with your decision.
D&C 8:10	• What is the most important thing we need to have when asking for something? (v. 10)	**trifle:** to not take seriously
D&C 9:8–9	• What does the Lord want us to do before we ask, and what do you think this means? (v. 8) • If our answer is right, how will we feel? (v. 8) • How will we feel if our answer is not right? (v. 9)	"Your bosom shall burn" usually means a feeling of peace. A "stupor of thought" often means you will feel confused and unsure about your decision. Steps: We need to have a *desire* to receive His help and we need to *believe* He will help us. It is important that we are *keeping the commandments* and *have an honest hear*t. We should also think about the question ourselves, and try to find the best answer we can. After we have done this, we need to pray if our answer is right. God answers us in different ways. We can have a thought in our minds or a feeling in our hearts. When we have made the right choice we will feel good and peaceful. Bad feelings or confusion let us know our decision is wrong.

LESSON SEVEN

The Three Witnesses

BACKGROUND

While Joseph and Oliver were translating the Book of Mormon, they read that three other people besides Joseph would be allowed to see the gold plates (see 2 Nephi 11:3; 27:12–14, Ether 5:2–4). Up until this time no other person had seen the gold plates, not even Joseph's wife and family. When Joseph would translate, there was either a blanket hung between him and his scribe, or the plates were covered with a cloth. When he wasn't translating, they were always covered.

Oliver Cowdery, Martin Harris, and David Whitmer felt inspired that they were to be the witnesses, and asked Joseph to inquire of the Lord. The Lord's answer is found in D&C 5 and 17.

WORD QUEST
- borne
- exalts

VERSES	SUGGESTED QUESTIONS	TREASURES OF KNOWLEDGE
D&C 5:1–3	• What did Martin Harris want to know for himself? (v. 1) • What covenant did Joseph make with the Lord? (v. 3) • What do you think would have happened if Joseph hadn't obeyed the Lord and had shown the plates to people? • How hard do you think it was for Joseph to not let anyone else, especially his wife and family, see the plates? • Joseph showed a great demonstration of faith and obedience to the Lord. Do you think you have that same faith and obedience? If not, what changes can you make to be more like Joseph?	**borne:** to give a witness of the truth
D&C 5:11–13	• How many witnesses would there be? (v. 11) • Who decided who the witnesses would be? (v. 11) • How would the witnesses know that these things are true? (vv. 12–13)	
D&C 5:23–26 (Note: These verses are referring to Martin Harris)	• What does the Lord tell Martin Harris he needs to do before he can see the plates? (v. 24) • What did the Lord command Martin to say after seeing the plates? (v. 25–26) • Why do you think it was important for Martin to testify to the world that he had seen the plates by the power of God and not of man?	**exalts:** to be proud (to think you know more than God or others)

VERSES	SUGGESTED QUESTIONS	TREASURES OF KNOWLEDGE
D&C 17:1–3	• Name five things the witnesses would be shown. (v. 1) • What did the witnesses need in order to see the plates? (v. 2) • What were the witnesses told to do after seeing the plates? (v. 3)	"The miraculous directors" refers to the liahona.
D&C 17:4–6	• Why was it necessary for the Lord to provide other witnesses besides Joseph? (v. 4) • In verse 6, the Lord gives His witness that the Book of Mormon is true. Why do you think this is important?	"One purpose of having the Three Witnesses … was to spread the burden of testifying among several individuals and, thus, protect the Prophet Joseph from being the single focus of the wrath of the world."*

* Stephen E. Robinson and H. Dean Garrett, *A Commentary on the Doctrine and Covenants* (Salt Lake City: Deseret Book, 2000), 1:99.

LESSON EIGHT

Witnesses See the Gold Plates

STORY

Not long after receiving the revelations found in D&C 5 and 17, Joseph Smith, Oliver Cowdery, Martin Harris, and David Whitmer went into the woods and prayed to see the plates. After several attempts at praying with no results, Martin Harris left the group. Martin felt responsible for them not receiving an answer since he had not completely repented after losing the manuscript. (Earlier that day, Joseph had told Martin that if he would repent of his sins, then God would allow him to be one of the Three Witnesses.)*

After Martin left, the angel Moroni appeared to Joseph Smith, Oliver Cowdery, and David Whitmer. He showed them the gold plates, the brass plates, the liahona, and the sword of Laban, along with other Nephite records.

They also heard a voice, declaring that the plates were "revealed by the power of God, and they have been translated by the power of God. The translation of them which you have seen is correct, and I command you to bear record of what you now see and hear."**

Afterwards Joseph went to find Martin Harris who was off by himself praying. Joseph and Martin prayed

* Joseph Smith. *History of The Church of Jesus Christ of Latter-day Saints.* Edited by B. H. Roberts. 2d ed. rev. 7 vols. (Salt Lake City: The Church of Jesus Christ of Latter-day Saints, 1932–51), 1:55.
** Ibid.

together, and soon Martin was privileged to see the same things.

Joseph was extremely relieved that other people were finally allowed to see the plates. He said to his parents, "I feel as if I was relieved of a burden which was almost too heavy for me to bear, and it rejoices my soul that I am not any longer to be entirely alone in the world."*

A few days later, Joseph was allowed to show eight additional men (Christian Whitmer, Jacob Whitmer, Peter Whitmer Jr., John Whitmer, Hiram Page, Joseph Smith Sr., Hyrum Smith, and Samuel H. Smith) the gold plates. The Eight Witnesses did not see an angel and were only shown the gold plates.

The Three Witnesses and the Eight Witnesses wrote their testimonies to the world that they had seen the gold plates and that they were real. Their testimonies can be found at the beginning of the Book of Mormon.

SUGGESTED QUESTIONS

- What do you think it must have been like for Joseph to not be able to show anyone else the plates?
- What are the names of the Three Witnesses?
- What were the Three Witnesses shown by the angel Moroni?
- Why did Martin Harris need to separate himself from the others? What does his situation teach you about receiving answers to prayers?
- Why do you think the Lord would only allow a few people to see the plates? Why didn't He let everyone see the plates?
- What was different between what the Three Witnesses and the Eight Witnesses saw?
- According to Elder Bruce R. McConkie, "A testimony consists of knowledge that comes by revelation.... [It] is received when the Holy Spirit speaks to the spirit within men. Receipt of a testimony is accompanied by a feeling of calm, unwavering certainty."** Why do you think the Lord wants us to gain a testimony by the Spirit and not by physical evidence?
- Can you think of any examples in the scriptures of someone who has seen a miracle, but did not remain faithful?

Optional: Read the testimonies of the Three Witnesses and the Eight Witnesses found at the beginning of the Book of Mormon. Discuss why these testimonies are important for the world to read.

* Joseph Smith. *History of The Church of Jesus Christ of Latter-day Saints*. Edited by B. H. Roberts. 2d ed. rev. 7 vols. (Salt Lake City: The Church of Jesus Christ of Latter-day Saints, 1932–51), 1:56.

** Bruce R. McConkie, *Mormon Doctrine* (Salt Lake City: Bookcraft, 1979), 785.

LESSON NINE

The Priesthood Restored

GOSPEL ART PICTURE KIT

407, 408

STORY

On May 15, 1829, while translating the Book of Mormon, Joseph and Oliver read about baptism and wanted to know more. They went into the woods to pray and ask the Lord about baptism. John the Baptist (from the New Testament) appeared and gave them the Aaronic Priesthood, which includes the power and authority to baptize.

The Aaronic Priesthood is the same priesthood given to the brother of Moses, whose name was Aaron. That is why it is called the Aaronic Priesthood.

John the Baptist needed to give the Aaronic Priesthood to Joseph and Oliver because no one living on the earth at that time held the authority of the priesthood. It had been gone from the earth since Jesus' apostles had died. And the only way to receive the priesthood is through someone else who has it.

The priesthood is the power and authority to act in the name of God. Since God cannot be with us here on earth, He allows men who are righteous to perform certain ordinances and blessings in His name and through His power.

John the Baptist commanded Joseph and Oliver that they should be baptized. "Accordingly we went and were baptized. I (Joseph Smith) baptized him first, and afterwards he baptized me—after which I laid my hands upon his head and ordained him to the Aaronic Priesthood, and afterwards he laid his hands on me and ordained me to the same Priesthood—for so we were commanded" (JS—H 1:71).

(Note: D&C 13 contains the words of John the Baptist to Joseph Smith and Oliver Cowdery. Optional: Read D&C 13)

Sometime later, Joseph and Oliver received the Melchizedek Priesthood from Peter, James, and John (Jesus' apostles from the New Testament). The Melchizedek Priesthood is named after a great man who lived in Old Testament times who held this priesthood. It was given the name Melchizedek to avoid the over use of the name of God, since we should only use His name when speaking reverently (see D&C 107:1–4).

The Melchizedek Priesthood is a higher priesthood, and gives men the authority to perform higher ordinances than the Aaronic Priesthood. Joseph needed to receive this priesthood before he could receive the gift of the Holy Ghost, organize the Church, and perform temple endowments.

SUGGESTED QUESTIONS

- When did Joseph and Oliver receive the Aaronic Priesthood?
- What is the name of the priesthood that John the Baptist gave to Joseph and Oliver, and where does the name come from?
- Why did John the Baptist need to give Joseph and Oliver the priesthood—why couldn't someone on earth do it?
- What did John the Baptist command Joseph and Oliver to do?
- Who did Joseph and Oliver receive the Melchizedek Priesthood from?
- Who is the Melchizedek Priesthood named after and why?
- What are some of the ordinances that can only be performed by someone holding the Melchizedek Priesthood?
- Because of the priesthood we are able to partake of the sacrament, be baptized, receive blessings, and have temples. Name some specific ways in which your life has been blessed because of the priesthood.

LESSON TEN

Serving in the Lord's Kingdom

BACKGROUND

During the early days of the Church, Joseph Smith received several revelations on behalf of other people who were seeking to know the Lord's will on how they could serve in His kingdom. The Lord's response to these men is found in D&C 4, 11, 12, 14, 15, and 16. These revelations all contain valuable counsel; however, this lesson will focus on D&C 11.

In May 1829, sometime after receiving the Aaronic Priesthood, Joseph's brother Hyrum asked Joseph to inquire of the Lord as to how he could best serve Him at this time. D&C 11 is the Lord's counsel to Hyrum Smith.

WORD QUEST

- heed
- dividing asunder
- revelation
- prophecy

VERSES	SUGGESTED QUESTIONS	TREASURES OF KNOWLEDGE
D&C 11:1–2	• What does God say is about to come forth, and what do you think this means? (v. 1) • How does God describe His word? (v. 2)	**heed:** to listen and pay attention **dividing asunder:** to separate "joints and marrow" refers to our "soul and spirit" (See D&C 33:1)
D&C 11:3–4	• Why do you think we will be blessed for teaching others about the gospel?	These verses are a reference to missionary work. There are many people in the world who are looking for the truth, and whoever wants, can help preach the Lord's gospel. Those who share the gospel will receive blessings in the next life.
D&C 11:5–7	• If you ask, you will ______; if you knock it shall ______. (v. 5) • What do you think it means to knock? • What does this verse teach you about receiving answers to prayer? • What two things does the Lord tell Hyrum to do? (v. 6)	
D&C 11:9, 12–13	• What counsel is Hyrum given? (v. 9) • What does the Spirit lead us to do? (v. 12) • What will the Lord's Spirit do for us? (v. 13)	

VERSES	SUGGESTED QUESTIONS	TREASURES OF KNOWLEDGE
D&C 11:18–20	• Name five things the Lord counseled Hyrum to do. (vv. 18–20) • How do you think we can keep the commandments with all our might, mind, and strength?	
D&C 11:21, 24–25	• What is Hyrum told to seek for, and what will happen if he does? (v. 21) • Why is it so important to know and understand the gospel before we can teach others? • What is the "rock"? (v. 24) • How can you know if your testimony is built on the rock? • Why is it important to believe in revelations?	**revelation:** "the making known of divine truth by communication from the heavens"* **prophecy:** "the inspired [words] of prophets"** "Build upon my rock": the foundation of our testimony needs to be built on the truth of Christ's gospel. If not, we will be like the foolish man who built his house upon the sand, and our testimonies could easily fall down.
D&C 11:28–30	• Who is Jesus Christ? (v. 28, 29) • What will the Lord give to those who receive Him and believe on His name? (v. 30)	"The life and the light of the world" is often used in the scriptures. Jesus Christ "is the light and life of the world because all things were made by him" (v. 28). He is the *light* of the world because He shows us the way back to Heavenly Father, and He "is the *life* of the world because his resurrection and his atonement save us from both physical and spiritual death."***

*James E. Talmage, *A Study of the Articles of Faith* (Salt Lake City: The Church of Jesus Christ of Latter-day Saints, 1947), 296.
** Bruce R. McConkie, *Mormon Doctrine* (Salt Lake City: Bookcraft, 1979), 602.
*** Dallin H. Oaks, "The Light and Life of the World," *Ensign*, November 1987, 63.

LESSON ELEVEN

Organization of the Church

BACKGROUND

When Joseph Smith and Oliver Cowdery received the Aaronic Priesthood from John the Baptist, they were told that the true church of Jesus Christ was to be organized for the first time since Jesus Christ was on the earth. They were given the exact date that the Church was to be organized: April 6, 1830.

Almost sixty people were in attendance at the organizational meeting in Peter Whitmer Sr.'s home in Fayette, New York. At this time there were only six people who had been baptized, the number needed to organize a new church according to New York State law. After the meeting several people were baptized, including Joseph's father, Joseph Smith Sr.

The name of the Church was not given at this time, but was given to Joseph at a later date as recorded in D&C 115:4.

D&C 20 is the Lord's instructions to this newly organized church, and contains both doctrines and teachings, along with duties and ordinances for Church members.

Note: This lesson contains two sections and can be studied separately, depending on the amount of time you wish to spend.

WORD QUEST

- Jew
- Gentile
- transgression
- sensual
- devilish
- crucified
- saved
- lest
- temptation
- broken heart
- contrite spirit
- remission
- sin

PART I—DOCTRINES OF THE CHURCH

VERSES	SUGGESTED QUESTIONS	TREASURES OF KNOWLEDGE
D&C 20:1–2	• On what date was the Church organized? (v. 1) • What was Joseph Smith called and ordained as? (v. 2)	President Spencer W. Kimball stated that April 6 is the date that Jesus Christ was born.*
D&C 20:8–11	• By what means did Joseph translate the Book of Mormon? (see footnote 8b) • What does the Book of Mormon contain, and who was it written for? (v. 9) • Who is verse 10 talking about? (see footnote 10b) • What does the truth of the Book of Mormon prove to the world (name three things)? (vv. 11–12)	**Jew:** usually referred to as those who are descendants of the kingdom of Judah (see Bible Dictionary, "Jew," 713). **Gentile:** often referred to as those who are not descendants of the house of Israel. (See Bible Dictionary, "Gentile," 679.)
D&C 20:17–19	• Name five truths about God that are taught in these verses. • Why is it important to know each of these truths and how can knowing those help you in your life?	"By these things" refers to the Book of Mormon. "Infinite and eternal" means that God goes on forever and has no end.

* Spencer W. Kimball, "Remarks and Dedication of the Fayette, New York, Buildings," *Ensign*, May 1980, 54.

VERSES	SUGGESTED QUESTIONS	TREASURES OF KNOWLEDGE
D&C 20:20–21	• Why did man become fallen? (v. 20) • What gift did God give to man? (v. 21)	These verses are referring to the transgression of Adam and Eve in the Garden of Eden. The term "fallen man" is a reference to our separation from God here on earth, and to our mortal bodies and desires. "Only Begotten Son": God is the father of our spirits, and our earthly father is the father of our bodies. However, God is the father of both Jesus' spirit and body. **transgression:** a broken commandment **sensual:** worldly, materialistic, and irreligious **devilish:** being like the devil
D&C 20:22–25	• Name three truths that are taught about Christ. (vv. 22–24) • What three things do we need to do in order to be saved? (v. 25)	**crucified:** to be put to death by being hung from a cross **saved:** to gain salvation (see "salvation" under "Treasures of Knowledge," p. 55).

VERSES	SUGGESTED QUESTIONS	TREASURES OF KNOWLEDGE
D&C 20:33, 37	• What do we need to do so we're not tempted? (v. 33) • Name five things we need to promise to do before we're baptized. (v. 37) • Why do you think each of these things is important to do before we make a covenant (a two-way promise) with God?	**lest:** in case **temptation:** to be influenced to do something you should not do **broken heart:** feeling bad for the things you have done wrong **contrite spirit:** having a desire to change and repent **remission:** forgiveness **sin:** to knowingly break a commandment When we take upon us the name of Christ, we gain access to His power, and we strive to become like Him.

PART II—DUTIES AND ORDINANCES OF THE CHURCH

Divide the family into three groups (mix older and younger members). Have each group choose a section of verses to read, and explain them to the rest of the family.

Group 1: Read verses 38–60

Explain to the family the different duties of an elder, a priest, a teacher, and a deacon.

Group 2: Read Verses 71–74 (GAK 601)

Explain to the family who can be baptized, and in what manner they are to be baptized.

Group 3: Read Verses 75–79 (GAK 603)

Explain to the family who can administer the sacrament. Also explain the promises we make when we take the sacrament, and what the Lord promises us in return. Challenge each family member to pay close attention the next time they listen to the sacrament prayers and to the promises they are making.

LESSON TWELVE

An Elect Lady

BACKGROUND

During the early days of the Church there were many people living around the Church members who disliked them because of their different beliefs. Many people were angry with the members and caused them a lot of suffering.

According to Joseph Smith, lies about him and his family were spread around: "The house was frequently beset by mobs and evil designing persons. Several times I was shot at, and very narrowly escaped … but the power and blessing of God attended me, and several began to believe my testimony."*

The persecution was hard for the early members who were trying to do the right thing by joining the Church and following the prophet. Joseph and Emma received the worst treatment by their enemies and she was often frightened for their lives. During this time, in July 1830, Joseph received a revelation from the Lord to his wife. This revelation (now D&C 25) comforted Emma and reminded her that the Lord knew her personally and was watching out for her and her family. Even though this revelation was given just for Emma, its important truths and teachings can apply to everyone (see verse 16).

WORD QUEST

- hearken
- virtue
- murmur
- console
- whithersoever
- expound
- exhort
- cleave
- meekness
- pride

GOSPEL ART PICTURE KIT

405

Joseph Smith. *History of The Church of Jesus Christ of Latter-day Saints.* Edited by B. H. Roberts. 2d ed. rev. 7 vols. (Salt Lake City: The Church of Jesus Christ of Latter-day Saints, 1932–51), 4:538.

VERSES	SUGGESTED QUESTIONS	TREASURES OF KNOWLEDGE
D&C 25:1–3	• Who are the sons and daughters of God's kingdom? (v. 1) • What does the Lord tell Emma she needs to do to receive an inheritance in Zion? (v. 2) • What did the Lord call Emma, and what do you think this means? (see footnote 3b)	**hearken:** listen and pay attention to **virtue:** goodness, righteousness Joseph Smith explained the phrase "elect lady" when Emma became the first president of the Relief Society on March 17, 1842. Joseph said that "elect meant to be elected to a certain work … and that the revelation was then fulfilled by Sister Emma's election to the Presidency of the Society."*
D&C 25:4–6	• What do you think Emma had not seen? (v. 4) • How do you think you would have felt if you were Joseph's wife and were not allowed to see the gold plates? • How did the Lord counsel Emma to treat her husband? (v. 5) • What did the Lord counsel Emma to do for Joseph and why? (v. 6) * Joseph Smith. *History of The Church of Jesus Christ of Latter-day Saints.* Edited by B.H. Roberts. 2d ed. rev. 7 vols. (Salt Lake City: The Church of Jesus Christ of Latter-day Saints, 1932–51), 4:552–553. ** Richard Lyman Bushman, *Joseph Smith: Rough Stone Rolling* (New York: Alfred A. Knopf, 2005) 57.	Even though Emma never saw the plates, they were never hidden from her. During the translation process they often sat on a table wrapped in a cloth. Emma said that she "felt of the plates … tracing their outline and shape. They seemed to be pliable like thick paper, and would rustle with a metallic sound."** **murmur:** to complain **console:** comfort **whithersoever:** to any place In September 1830, the Lord sent Oliver Cowdery on a mission to preach the gospel to the Lamanites (the American Indians; see D&C 28:8).

VERSES	SUGGESTED QUESTIONS	TREASURES OF KNOWLEDGE
D&C 25:7–9	• What was Emma ordained to do? (v. 7) • How was Emma to spend her time? (v. 8) • What was Joseph Smith's calling? (v. 9)	**expound:** to explain **exhort:** to encourage Joseph Smith's first responsibility was to lead the Church. Emma's fears were that Joseph would not be able to provide for their family. But the Lord promised He would take care of their needs through the Church and its members.
D&C 25:10–12	• What counsel does the Lord give Emma, and what do you think this means? (v. 10) • What is Emma told to do? (v. 11) • How does the Lord feel about righteous songs? (v. 12)	Having things of the world are only wrong when we want them more than we want the things of God. Our hearts and desires should be focused on seeking for the "things of a better world"—things that will draw us closer to God and His kingdom.
D&C 25:13–16	• Name six things Emma is counseled to do. (v. 13–15) • What is Emma promised if she follows the Lord's counsel? (v. 15) • Who else does this section apply to? (v. 16) * Hoyt W. Brewster Jr., *Doctrine and Covenants Encyclopedia* (Salt Lake City: Deseret Book, 1988), 115.	**cleave:** to remain faithful **meekness:** humble, patient, calm **pride:** to think you know more or what is better for you than God does "Crown of righteousness": "Just as the heads of royalty on earth wear crowns to signify their stature, so will celestial kings and queens, figuratively, if not literally, wear crowns symbolic of their royal stature, dominion, and authority."*

LESSON THIRTEEN

Gifts of the Spirit

BACKGROUND

In September 1830 the Lord sent missionaries to the West to preach the gospel to the American Indians. On their way the missionaries stopped in Kirtland, Ohio, to preach the gospel. They met a preacher named Sidney Rigdon who joined the Church. Many members of Sidney's congregation were also baptized (hundreds of people joined the Church in Kirtland in the first few months).

Sidney Rigdon later came to New York to meet the Prophet Joseph Smith. In December 1830 the Lord told Joseph that the Saints needed to move to Ohio (over 250 miles away). The Lord told him that they would receive His law and would "be endowed with power from on high" (see D&C 38:32), which are blessings of the temple.

Many of the Church members followed the Lord's counsel and sold their homes and farms. Between February and May 1831, the majority of the New York Saints left their homes and moved to Ohio.

During the early days of the Church there were many members who received visions and gifts from the Spirit. However, some visions and gifts were not from God. Section 46 was given to the Church so that members would know the difference between the true Spirit of the Lord and false spirits.

WORD QUEST
- seduced
- deceived
- earnestly
- profited

GOSPEL ART PICTURE KIT

418

VERSES	SUGGESTED QUESTIONS	TREASURES OF KNOWLEDGE
D&C 46:7–10	• Name three things we can so that we are not "seduced by evil spirits." (v. 7) • What are we to seek earnestly for? (v. 8) • Who are the gifts of the Spirit given to? (v. 9) • What should we always remember? (v. 10)	**seduced:** to be led astray **deceived:** to believe something that is not true **earnestly:** sincerely and with effort "All inspiration does not come from God.... There are promptings from evil sources which are so carefully counterfeited as to deceive even the very elect. Nevertheless, we can learn to discern these spirits."*
D&C 46:11–12	• Is everyone given a gift? (v. 11) • Why do people have different gifts? (v. 12)	**profited:** to gain something
D&C 46:13–14	• What two gifts are mentioned in these verses? • Why is it important to have these gifts? (v. 14)	
D&C 46:17–26	• Name eight gifts that are given to people. Talk about each gift and how that gift would benefit others.	The gift of the word of wisdom is not the same as the revelation in D&C 89. This gift refers to being wise, which is having both knowledge and judgment. The gift of discerning spirits is the ability to tell if something is from God or not. The gift of tongues is the ability to speak and understand different languages.

* Boyd K. Packer, "Revelation in a Changing World," *Ensign*, November 1989, 14.

VERSES	SUGGESTED QUESTIONS	TREASURES OF KNOWLEDGE
D&C 46:28–30	• How do we receive these gifts? (v. 28) • Who do you think has all those gifts? (v. 29) • When we ask in the Spirit, we ask according to what? And what will happen? (v. 30)	
D&C 46:31–33	• In whose name and by what power do these gifts come? (v. 31) • What should we remember to do? (v. 32) • What do we need to practice continually? (v. 33)	To practice virtue and holiness continually means we are always trying our best to be good and to be like God.

LESSON FOURTEEN

Blessings of Keeping the Commandments

BACKGROUND

In June 1831, Joseph Smith was told by the Lord that some of the Saints would need to move to Independence, Missouri, over one thousand miles from Kirtland, Ohio. The Lord revealed to Joseph that Jackson County, Missouri, is the place where the Lord would establish Zion and where a temple would be built.

The Saints sought to establish Zion, a place where they could live together with "one heart and one mind, and (dwell) in righteousness … [with] no poor among them" (Moses 7:18), and where Jesus Christ will come and reign during the Second Coming (see D&C 101:70–71 and Article of Faith 1:10).

In August 1831, Joseph received D&C 59 on behalf of the Saints who were living in Missouri, and who were desirous to establish a Zion society among them.

WORD QUEST

- adultery
- oblations
- raiment
- extortion
- offend
- wrath
- kindled

VERSES	SUGGESTED QUESTIONS	TREASURES OF KNOWLEDGE
D&C 59:5–6	• Name five commandments that are given. (vv. 5–6) • What do you think it means to love God with all our heart, might, mind, and strength? (v. 5) • Who are our neighbors and how can we show them our love? (v. 6)	**adultery:** the breaking of the marriage covenant
D&C 59:7–8	• What two commandments are given? (vv. 7–8) • Why do you think it's important to give thanks?	A sacrifice is the giving of something. A "sacrifice…in righteousness" is the giving of ourselves—the promise to obey all that the Lord asks us to do.
D&C 59:9–10, 12	• How do you keep yourself unspotted from the world? (v. 9) • What types of activities are appropriate on Sundays? (vv. 10, 12)	**oblations:** an offering, such as our service, our thanks, or our money to God. "Unspotted from the world" means to not become worldly in our dress, actions, attitudes, or beliefs. "In this day of increasing access to and preoccupation with materialism, there is a sure protection for ourselves and our children… The key to that sure protection surprisingly can be found in Sabbath observance."*

* James E. Faust, "The Lord's Day," *Ensign*, November 1991, 33.

VERSES	SUGGESTED QUESTIONS	TREASURES OF KNOWLEDGE
D&C 59:13–15	• How should we prepare our meals, and what do you think this means? (v. 13) • What attitude should we have in keeping the Sabbath day holy? (v. 14, 15)	"Let thy food be prepared with singleness of heart" means that we don't let the preparation of the meal occupy our thoughts and hearts—they should be focused on the things of the Spirit. The phrase "not with much laughter" refers to too much or inappropriate laughter—such as making fun of sacred things or teasing others.
D&C 59:16–19	• How will we be blessed if we keep the Sabbath day holy? (v. 16) • The things of the earth are made for what purpose? (vv. 18–19)	**raiment:** clothing
D&C 59:20–21	• What pleases God? (v. 20) • What offends God? (v. 21) • Why do you think it offends God when we're not thankful? • What are some blessings that God has given you that you are thankful for?	**extortion:** by force or violence **offend:** to cause displeasure **wrath:** strong displeasure **kindled:** to stir up an emotion "Confess not his hand" means that we don't acknowledge and give thanks to God for all He does for us.
D&C 59:23–24	• What will be our reward if we are righteous? (v. 23) • How important is it to you to have peace in your life? • Are there changes you can make to be more righteous and receive more peace?	

LESSON FIFTEEN

The Three Degrees of Glory

BACKGROUND

In June 1830, Joseph was commanded by the Lord to make important changes in the Bible. Joseph was told that many truths had been lost or removed from the Bible over the years, which changed the meaning of some scripture and confused the truth.

Joseph worked on these changes for three years. During this time he would often have questions for the Lord that resulted in revelations that are now contained in the Doctrine and Covenants.

On February 16, 1832, while reading John's Gospel in the Bible, Joseph wrote, "It was apparent that many important points touching the salvation of man had been taken from the Bible, or lost before it was compiled. It appeared self-evident from what truths were left, that if God rewarded every one according to the deeds done in the body, the term 'Heaven,' as intended for the Saints' eternal home, must include more kingdoms than one. Accordingly, while translating St. John's Gospel, myself and Elder Rigdon saw the following vision" (D&C 76 heading).

Joseph Smith and Sidney Rigdon (who was assisting him) received several visions that are recorded in D&C 76.

D&C 76, referred to by the early Saints as "The Vision," revealed doctrine of the three degrees of glory that resurrected spirits will be assigned to in the next life, after the millennium, and after the final judgment.

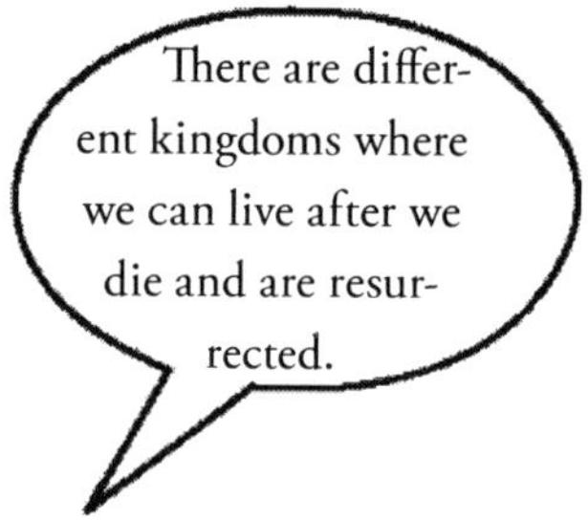

WORD QUEST

- transcendent
- firmament
- honorable
- valiant
- sorcerer
- whoremonger
- surpasses

Note: This lesson will focus only on the three kingdoms; however, parents are encouraged to read through any additional verses they feel their family would benefit from.

This lesson contains three sections and can be studied separately, depending on the amount of time you wish to spend.

PART I—THE CELESTIAL KINGDOM

VERSES	SUGGESTED QUESTIONS	TREASURES OF KNOWLEDGE
D&C 76:11–12	• Who received the vision and on what date was it received? (v. 11) • By what power did they receive the vision? (v. 12)	
D&C 76:70, 51–52	• What is celestial glory like? (v. 70) • Name five requirements for obtaining a celestial glory? (vv. 51–52)	"Whose bodies are celestial": "In the resurrection, our bodies will receive glory appropriate to those principles by which we lived during our probation.… What we seek to live here, we will receive there."*
D&C 76:62–64	• Where will the righteous dwell? (v. 62) • What two future events will the righteous be a part of? (vv. 63–64)	The first resurrection is the period between the Savior's resurrection and the end of the millennium. All who are righteous will be resurrected sometime during this period.
D&C 137:1–4	• What kingdom did Joseph see? (v. 1) • Who did Joseph see? (v. 3) • Describe the gate and the streets. (v. 2, 4)	**transcendent:** beyond our mortal understanding

* Stephen E. Robinson and H. Dean Garrett, *A Commentary on the Doctrine and Covenants* (Salt Lake City: Deseret Book, 2000), 2:313.

PART II—THE TERRESTRIAL KINGDOM

VERSES	SUGGESTED QUESTIONS	TREASURES OF KNOWLEDGE
D&C 76:71–76	• The glory of the celestial is compared to the sun. The glory of the terrestrial is compared to what? (v. 71) • How are the sun and the moon different from each other and how do you think this relates to the differences between the celestial and terrestrial glories? • Describe five types of people who will receive a terrestrial glory. (vv. 72–76)	**firmament:** the sky **honorable:** honest, fair, and good "The full glory of God is much, much greater than the energy of the sun. The relative glories of the sun, moon, and stars are only symbolic of the differences between the heavenly kingdoms."* The "church of the Firstborn" refers to the church of Jesus Christ, since he is the firstborn spirit of the Father. "Blinded by the craftiness of men" means that the things of the world were more of an influence in how someone believed and acted than the gospel of Jesus Christ was.
D&C 76:77–78	• What will terrestrial beings receive? (v. 77) • What will terrestrial beings not receive, and what do you think this means? (v. 77) • How do you think you would feel if you lived in the terrestrial kingdom and why?	

*Stephen E. Robinson and H. Dean Garrett, *A Commentary on the Doctrine and Covenants* (Salt Lake City: Deseret Book, 2000), 2:313.

VERSES	SUGGESTED QUESTIONS	TREASURES OF KNOWLEDGE
D&C 76:79–80	• What will happen to those who are not valiant in the testimony of Jesus, and what do you think this means? (v. 79)	**valiant:** not afraid to act Those "who are not valiant in the testimony of Jesus" are those who have testimonies and "belong to the Church but do not magnify their callings in the priesthood, act diligently, pay their tithing, honor the Sabbath day, and the like.… Such persons are 'lukewarm, and neither cold nor hot.' "*

PART III—THE TELESTIAL KINGDOM

VERSES	SUGGESTED QUESTIONS	TREASURES OF KNOWLEDGE
D&C 76:81	• The glory of the telestial is compared to what? (v. 81)	
D&C 76:82,103–104	• Name five types of people who will receive a telestial glory.	**sorcerer:** someone who practices dark magic **whoremonger:** a prostitute's customer

* Bruce R. McConkie, *Mormon Doctrine* (Salt Lake City: Bookcraft, 1979), 820.

VERSES	SUGGESTED QUESTIONS	TREASURES OF KNOWLEDGE
D&C 76:84–85	• What will happen to those who receive a telestial glory?	"Hell," for the wicked, is the time period between death and the resurrection. Hell "will have an end, when all the captive spirits have paid the price of their sins and enter into a degree of glory of their resurrection" (Bible Dictionary, "Hell," 700). The last resurrection will take place after the millennium.
D&C 76:89, 91	• The glory of the telestial surpasses what, and what do you think this means? (v. 89) • If the glory of the telestial is greater than we can imagine, then what do you think the glory of the terrestrial and celestial kingdom are like? • The glory of the terrestrial is greater than which kingdom? (v. 91)	**surpasses:** beyond our ability to comprehend "The lowest glory to which man is assigned is so glorious as to be beyond the understanding of man… The meanest sinner, in the final judgment, will receive a glory which is beyond human understanding.… The Gospel is a gospel of tremendous love. Love is at the bottom of it."*
D&C 76:92	• Which kingdom does God live in? (v. 92) • Which kingdom has the most glory? (v. 92) • Which kingdom do you want to live in, and why? • What can you do now to help you get there?	

* *Doctrine and Covenants Student Manual* (Salt Lake City: The Church of Jesus Christ of Latter-day Saints, 2001), 166.

LESSON SIXTEEN

The Word of Wisdom

BACKGROUND

While living in Kirtland, Ohio, Joseph started the School of the Prophets under the direction of the Lord. (See D&C 88:127–141). The school was held above Newel K. Whitney's store where Joseph and Emma lived. The school provided instruction to the leaders of the Church in such areas as gospel doctrine, Church business, and missionary work.

Often while the men were meeting, they would smoke and chew tobacco (the harmful effects of such were unknown at this time). The room often smelled of smoke and the floor was dirty; Joseph felt that this was not right, and inquired of the Lord as to how to handle the situation. In answer to his prayer, Joseph received D&C 89.

This counsel from the Lord was not officially made a commandment until eighteen years later when, during general conference, President Brigham Young asked the Saints to make a covenant to live by the Word of Wisdom. From that time on it became a commandment for all Church members to live by.

WORD QUEST
- constitution
- prudence

VERSES	SUGGESTED QUESTIONS	TREASURES OF KNOWLEDGE
D&C 89:1, 5	• Who is the Word of Wisdom for? (v. 1) • What are we counseled not to drink? (v. 5)	"Strong drink" means alcoholic drinks.
D&C 89:7–9	• Name three things that are not for the belly. (vv. 7–9)	"Hot drinks" means tea and coffee. "The Word of Wisdom is a key to individual revelation.… If we abuse our body with habit-forming substances, or misuse prescription drugs, we draw curtains which close off the light of spiritual communication."*
D&C 89:10–12	• What is the purpose of wholesome herbs? (v. 10) • How are we to use herbs and fruits? (v. 11) • What has the Lord ordained (given) for the use of man? (v. 12)	**constitution:** the physical make up of the body **prudence:** good judgment "Wholesome herbs" means all vegetation that we can eat. They were created for the health and benefit of our bodies.
D&C 89:14, 17	• What is grain ordained for? (v. 14) • Name five grains listed, and who or what they are made for. (v. 17)	

* Boyd K. Packer, "Revelation in a Changing World," *Ensign*, November 1989, 14.

VERSES	SUGGESTED QUESTIONS	TREASURES OF KNOWLEDGE
D&C 89:18–21	• Name four blessings that the Saints will receive for obeying the Word of Wisdom. (vv. 18–21) • Why would you want to receive each of these blessings?	"Health in the navel, marrow in the bones": navel refers to the inside of our bodies, and marrow refers to strength and vitality. Thus, those who keep the word of wisdom will be healthier and have more strength and energy than those who do not. "The destroying angel shall pass by them" is a reference to the promise given to Moses and the children of Israel while in bondage to the Egyptians; when on a certain night God took the life of all the firstborn in Egypt except for those who put blood on their doors. However, "it is not from mortal death that we shall be spared in such a passover… But there is spiritual death which you need not suffer… If you are obedient."* (Spiritual death is separation from God and His influence.)

* Boyd K. Packer, "The Word of Wisdom: The Principle and the Promises," *Ensign*, May 1996, 17.

LESSON SEVENTEEN

Persecution of the Saints in Missouri

GOSPEL ART PICTURE KIT:

409

STORY

In the summer of 1831 some of the Saints began to settle in Jackson County, Missouri. By 1832 there were more than eight hundred Saints living there and problems began to arise. Some Church members were not listening to their local Church leaders, and others criticized the Prophet. There was also fighting, arguing, jealousy, and unbelief among some of the Saints.

Problems also arose with the local settlers in Jackson County. Most of the settlers were uneducated, believed in slavery, feared the American Indians, and had different political views from the Mormons. The Saints were mostly educated, believed in freeing the slaves, and were friendly with the American Indians.

The differences in how the Saints and the local citizens lived brought tension. According to Joseph Smith, "We could not associate with our neighbors... in their midnight revels, their Sabbath breaking, horse

* Joseph Smith. *History of The Church of Jesus Christ of Latter-day Saints.* Edited by B. H. Roberts. 2d ed. rev. 7 vols. (Salt Lake City: The Church of Jesus Christ of Latter-day Saints, 1932–51), 4:538.

racing, and gambling; they commenced at first to ridicule, then to persecute, and finally an organized mob assembled."*

Along with the differences in lifestyle, many Saints bragged about being God's chosen people and said they were there in Jackson County to build up Zion, which, they said, would only include Church members. This of course upset the local Missourians, as well as the ministers of other local churches. Many ministers were angry about the Church's teachings and were afraid that they would lose people from their churches, so some of them spread fear and lies about the Saints.

These and other issues made the people of Missouri angry with the Mormons. On July 20, 1833, over three hundred Missourians met together to draft a document that would force the Mormons to leave the county. The mob took the document to Church leaders who refused to sign it. This angered the mob and as a result they destroyed the home and printing press of W. W. Phelps. At this time Brother Phelps was working on printing copies of the Book of Commandments (which contained many of the revelations now contained in the Doctrine and Covenants).

Two young girls, Mary Elizabeth and Caroline Rollins, saved pages from the printing press, ran into the fields, laid on top of the pages, and hid from the mobs.

Bishop Edward Partridge and a man named Charles Allen were dragged into the street during the mob attack and tarred and feathered. This means that hot tar was poured onto their bare skin and the feathers were scattered on top of the hot tar.

On July 23, 1833, the mob came again and told Church leaders that they would attack the Church members if the leaders did not sign a paper stating that they would all leave the county by January 1, 1834. Reluctantly, Church leaders signed the document out of fear for the lives of the Saints.

Upon hearing about the persecution of the Missouri Saints, Joseph Smith counseled them to seek legal action against the forcibly signed document. This caused the mob leaders to fear that the Saints would not keep their promise to leave the county, so between October 31, and November 4, 1833, the mob attacked and forced over one thousand Saints from their homes. Many women and children were made to walk in the cold, snowy weather to other counties in Missouri. Joseph Smith later reported that hundreds of Saints "houseless and homeless, had to wander on the bleak prairies till the children left the tracks of their blood on the prairie."*

Most of the Saints ended up in Clay County, Missouri, where they found shelter and protection. The Saints never returned to their homes in Jackson County.

* Joseph Smith. *History of The Church of Jesus Christ of Latter-day Saints.* Edited by B. H. Roberts. 2d ed. rev. 7 vols. (Salt Lake City: The Church of Jesus Christ of Latter-day Saints, 1932–51), 4:539.

SUGGESTED QUESTIONS

- Name three reasons why the local Missourians were upset with the Mormon people.
- What type of document did the mob want Church leaders to sign?
- What did the mob do to W. W. Phelps, along with his home and printing press?
- What was Brother Phelps printing at that time, and what happened to the copies?
- Why did Church leaders finally agree to sign the mob's document?
- Why did the mob attack the Saints again in October and November 1833?
- What did the mob do to the Saints?
- When the mob attacked, where did the Saints go?
- How do you think you would have felt if you had been a member of the Church living in Missouri at this time?
- What can you learn from the Saints' example about having faith and courage even during difficult times?

LESSON EIGHTEEN

Affliction in Zion

BACKGROUND

Before giving this lesson, read the story "Persecution of the Saints in Missouri." After he heard about the persecution of the Saints in Missouri, Joseph Smith (who was living in Kirtland, Ohio) received revelations that are now D&C 101 and 103.

WORD QUEST

- consequence
- chastened
- sanctified
- jarrings
- strifes
- esteemed
- mourned
- redemption
- grievous
- precepts
- salvation
- impart

VERSES	SUGGESTED QUESTIONS	TREASURES OF KNOWLEDGE
D&C 101:1–2	• Why did the Lord allow the Saints to be persecuted? (v. 2)	**consequence:** because of
D&C 101:4–5	• Who does the Lord compare the Saints' trial to? (v. 4) • What will happen if we lose faith because of our trials? (v. 5)	**chastened:** to be corrected by punishment **sanctified:** made holy
D&C 101:6–8	• Name five of the Saints transgressions. (v. 6) • Why did the Lord not answer their prayers right away? (v. 7) • How do you think the Lord feels when we only come to Him for help during our trials? (v. 8)	**jarrings:** quarrels or disagreements **strifes:** fighting **esteemed:** to respect If, when our lives are filled with peace, we don't follow God's counsel, then when times of trial come, we should not expect to easily find His help.
D&C 101:9, 13–14	• Despite the Saints' transgressions, how did the Lord feel toward them? (v. 9) • What does the Lord say will happen to those who have been scattered by the mobs, and for those who mourn? (vv. 13–14) • Have you ever felt comforted by the Lord when you were sad? If so, describe your experience and how it made you feel.	**mourned:** to feel grief or sorrow

VERSES	SUGGESTED QUESTIONS	TREASURES OF KNOWLEDGE
D&C 103:1, 4	• Why were the Saints chastened? (v. 4)	**redemption:** deliverance from the consequences of sin **grievous:** great pain or suffering **precepts:** laws **salvation:** life with God in the celestial kingdom "To gain salvation—means to be saved from spiritual and physical death." Everyone will receive salvation from physical death, but salvation from spiritual death is conditioned on our righteousness. However, in most instances the term "salvation" is referring to the spiritual death, and the receiving of exaltation, which is living in "the highest state of happiness and glory in the celestial realm."*
D&C 103:9–10	• The Saints were set to be what, and what do you think this means? (v. 9) • The Lord compares the Saints to what? (v. 10) • Why do you think we're not useful to the Lord when we lose our savor? (see Treasures of Knowledge)	Salt is used for preserving and healing. When salt has savor it is pure and useful. Salt loses its savor through "mixture and contamination."* When salt loses its savor it is useless, good for nothing, and thrown out. We lose our savor, our purity, when we become wicked and worldly.

* Russell M. Nelson, "Salvation and Exaltation," *Ensign*, May 2008, 7–10.
* Carlos E. Asay, "Salt of the Earth: Savor of Men and Saviors of Men," *Ensign*, 1980, 42.

VERSES	SUGGESTED QUESTIONS	TREASURES OF KNOWLEDGE
D&C 105:1–3	• What were the Saints doing that was wrong? (v. 3)	**impart:** give
D&C 105:4–6	• Zion must be built on what principles? (v. 5) • What did the Lord want the Saints to learn through their chastening? (v. 6) • Have each family member name one thing they learned from the Saints experiences with afflictions that can help them in their own trials.	

LESSON NINETEEN

Priesthood Duties

BACKGROUND

In February 1835, in Kirtland, Ohio, Twelve Apostles of the Lord Jesus Christ were chosen in the Latter-days. In March 1835, it was decided that the members of the Twelve would leave Kirtland and go on missions to preach the gospel. Before leaving on their missions, they sought the counsel of the Lord. “The time when we are about to separate is near; and when we shall meet again, God only knows; we therefore feel to ask … our Prophet and Seer, that he inquire of God for us … that we may look upon it when we are separated, that our hearts may be comforted.”*

Joseph Smith inquired of the Lord on behalf of the departing apostles and received what is now D&C 107.

WORD QUEST

- appendage
- upheld
- especial
- aspire
- dominion
- compulsion
- unfeigned
- hypocrisy
- guile
- scepter

* Joseph Smith. *History of The Church of Jesus Christ of Latter-day Saints.* Edited by B.H. Roberts. 2d ed. rev. 7 vols. (Salt Lake City: The Church of Jesus Christ of Latter-day Saints, 1932–51), 2:210.

VERSES	SUGGESTED QUESTIONS	TREASURES OF KNOWLEDGE
D&C 107:1–4	• What are the names of the two priesthoods in the Church? (v. 1) • What was the priesthood called before Melchizedek? (v. 3) • Why was the name of the priesthood changed to the Melchizedek Priesthood? (v. 4)	"The terms *Aaronic* and *Levitical* [Priesthoods] are sometimes used synonymously." It has two names because they had different responsibilities in the times of Moses (see Bible Dictionary, "Aaronic Priesthood," 599).
D&C 107:13–14	• Why is the second priesthood called after Aaron? (v. 13) • Why is it called the lesser priesthood? (v. 14)	**appendage:** a part that is joined to something larger
D&C 107:18–20	• Name four blessings that come from having the power and authority of the Melchizedek priesthood. (vv. 18–19) • What power and authority do those with the Aaronic priesthood have? (v. 20)	Joseph Smith stated that the Melchizedek Priesthood "is the channel through which all knowledge, doctrine, the plan of salvation, and every important matter is revealed from heaven."*
D&C 107:21–22	• How many High Priests are in the Presidency of the Church? (v. 22) • The First Presidency is upheld by what? (v. 22) • Who is currently in the First Presidency of the Church?	**upheld:** supported

* Joseph Smith. *History of The Church of Jesus Christ of Latter-day Saints*. Edited by B. H. Roberts. 2d ed. rev. 7 vols. (Salt Lake City: The Church of Jesus Christ of Latter-day Saints, 1932–51), 4:207.

VERSES	SUGGESTED QUESTIONS	TREASURES OF KNOWLEDGE
D&C 107:25–26	• What are the Seventy called to do? (v. 25) • The authority of the Seventy is equal to what? (v. 26) • How many of the current members of the Seventy can you name? (Hint: Look in the latest conference edition of the *Ensign*.)	**especial:** of special importance or significance

Note: The following verses were given to Joseph Smith when he was held prisoner in Liberty Jail. These verses contain important counsel to priesthood holders in how they should use the priesthood.

VERSES	SUGGESTED QUESTIONS	TREASURES OF KNOWLEDGE
D&C 121:34–36	• Why are some men not chosen? (v. 35) • The rights of the priesthood are connected to what, and can only be controlled by what? (v. 36) • What do you think these verses mean?	**aspire:** to seek or accomplish a goal "The power of the priesthood is the authority to act for God. Therefore, those who hold the priesthood are empowered to do *only* what God would do in a given situation."*

* Stephen E. Robinson and H. Dean Garrett, *A Commentary on the Doctrine and Covenants* (Salt Lake City: Deseret Book, 2000), 4:160–61.

VERSES	SUGGESTED QUESTIONS	TREASURES OF KNOWLEDGE
D&C 121:37, 40	• Name four things that cause men to lose the authority of the priesthood. (v. 37) • Why do you think each of these things would cause the Lord to be grieved?	**dominion:** control or power over another **compulsion:** using force to cause something to happen The phrases "gratify pride" and "vain ambition" refer to seeking out worldly success that is focused on our selfish needs and desires and not on serving other people. "Amen to the priesthood" means one will lose the power and authority of the priesthood that they hold. A person cannot expect to act in the name of God when he acts contrary to the laws and nature of God.
D&C 121:41–42	• Name seven ways a man with the priesthood should act toward those he is in authority over. (vv. 41–42)	**unfeigned:** genuine, sincere **hypocrisy:** pretending to have moral or religious character that one does not really possess **guile:** to deceive or trick someone into doing what you want

VERSES	SUGGESTED QUESTIONS	TREASURES OF KNOWLEDGE
D&C 121:43, 45–46	• When a priesthood holder needs to correct someone, what should he do? (v. 43) • What do these verses teach you about the importance of being a righteous priesthood holder? • How should we, and priesthood holders, feel toward others? (v. 45) • Why do you think it's important to have good, pure thoughts all the time? • Why do you think it's important for priesthood holders to have the Holy Ghost with them?	**scepter:** a symbol of power and authority "Reproving betimes with sharpness" means to "reprove in such a way that the reproved person clearly knows wherein he has erred. Sharpness does not necessarily relate to one's tone of voice."* "Let virtue garnish thy thoughts unceasingly": we should always have good and righteous thoughts. "Confidence wax strong in the presence of God": if we are righteous and follow the commandments of God, we will have a desire to be in His presence one day. "Distil upon thy soul as the dews from heaven": "As the dews from heaven come quietly and gently … in the early hours of the morning, so we are promised that the doctrine of the priesthood will come quietly and without fanfare as we learn and practice the lessons taught in verses 35–45."**

* Hoyt W. Brewster Jr., *Doctrine and Covenants Encyclopedia* (Salt Lake City: Deseret Book, 1988), 461.

** Stephen E. Robinson and H. Dean Garrett, *A Commentary on the Doctrine and Covenants* (Salt Lake City: Deseret Book, 2000), 4:166.

LESSON TWENTY

The Kirtland Temple

GOSPEL ART PICTURE KIT

500

STORY

There were two main groups of Saints during the early days of the Church. One group was in Missouri, and the other was in Kirtland, Ohio, where Joseph Smith resided.

In December 1832, Joseph was told by the Lord to build a temple in Kirtland (D&C 88:119). However, by June 1, 1833, the Kirtland Saints had not started the temple. On that day, Joseph Smith received a revelation from the Lord chastising the Saints for their delay in building His house (see D&C 95:3). Immediately upon receiving this revelation (now section 95), the Saints began building the temple.

The First Presidency of the Church (Joseph Smith, Sidney Rigdon, and Fredrick G. Williams) was shown in a vision how the temple should look. In D&C 95 the Lord gave instructions on the size and purpose of the temple (D&C 95:15–17).

The Kirtland Saints were very poor, and it took a lot of sacrifice to finish the temple. All the Saints took part in the building of the temple by donating their money, their time, and their goods.

Joseph Smith stated that even though "the Church was poor, yet our unity, harmony and charity abounded to strengthen us to do the commandments of God."*

The women made clothes for the workers and curtains to hang in the finished temple. They also sacrificed their china dishes and glasses to be crushed and added to the outside plaster, which made the walls of the temple shine.

On March 27, 1836, three years after construction began, the Kirtland Temple was dedicated. When a temple is dedicated, it becomes a holy place. It is set apart from the world as a place where the Lord can come and reveal His word to His people, and where His people can make sacred covenants with Him. A dedicated temple that is "kept holy … symbolizes or represents a part of the celestial kingdom upon the earth, and communion between the Saints and their God can take place."**

Joseph Smith offered the dedicatory prayer (D&C 109), which is a prayer given by the prophet to the Lord in which the temple is officially set apart as a house of the Lord.

At the Kirtland Temple dedication, the Saints sang "The Spirit of God." This song was written by W. W. Phelps for this event and is still sung at temple dedications today.

Many Saints witnessed miracles and saw glorious visions during the weeks before the temple was completed, during the temple dedication, and for weeks after. On the evening of the dedication, "a noise was heard like the sound of a rushing mighty wind, which filled the Temple."*** Other Saints testified that they had seen visions and angels, and "the people of the neighborhood … [saw] a bright light like a pillar of fire resting upon the Temple."****

This was a glorious time for the Kirtland Saints who had spent their time, talents, and money on sacrificing to build a house to their God. Through these experiences the Lord blessed and strengthened these faithful Saints.

The Kirtland Temple was not used for all the same purposes that our modern-day temples are used for today. It housed the offices of the Church leadership, was a place where meetings for Church leaders could be held, where the School of the Prophets was held, and where some temple ordinances were given. The full temple ordinances that take place today were not performed by the Saints until the Nauvoo Temple was completed in 1845.

* Joseph Smith. *History of The Church of Jesus Christ of Latter-day Saints.* Edited by B. H. Roberts. 2d ed. rev. 7 vols. (Salt Lake City: The Church of Jesus Christ of Latter-day Saints, 1932–51), 1:349.

** Stephen E. Robinson and H. Dean Garrett, *A Commentary on the Doctrine and Covenants* (Salt Lake City: Deseret Book, 2000), 4:44.

*** Joseph Smith. *History of The Church of Jesus Christ of Latter-day Saints.* Edited by B. H. Roberts. 2d ed. rev. 7 vols. (Salt Lake City: The Church of Jesus Christ of Latter-day Saints, 1932–51), 2:428.

**** Ibid., 2:428.

SUGGESTED QUESTIONS

- When did the Kirtland Saints begin to build a temple?
- How did they know what the temple should look like?
- What kinds of sacrifices did the Saints make in building the temple?
- How long did it take to build the temple?
- What does it mean to dedicate a temple?
- On what date was the Kirtland Temple dedicated?
- What song did the Saints sing at the temple dedication?
- What did some of the Saints see at the temple dedication?
- Why do you think the Saints were given such glorious visions at the temple dedication?
- What does the story of the building of the Kirtland Temple teach you about sacrificing your needs for the Lord?

LESSON TWENTY-ONE

Priesthood Keys Are Restored

BACKGROUND

Read "The Kirtland Temple" story before giving this lesson.

On April 3, 1836, the Sunday after the Kirtland Temple was dedicated, a meeting was held in the temple. After the sacrament was administered to the congregation, Joseph Smith and Oliver Cowdery went behind one of the veils in the temple (long curtains that were used to separate sections of the temple) and knelt in prayer. After praying, both Joseph and Oliver were shown a series of visions that are recorded in D&C 110.

GOSPEL ART PICTURE KIT

417

WORD QUEST

- veil
- advocate
- pollute
- keys
- dispensation

VERSES	SUGGESTED QUESTIONS	TREASURES OF KNOWLEDGE
D&C 110:1–3	• Who did Joseph and Oliver see? (v. 2) • Describe what He looked like and where He was standing. (vv. 2–3)	**veil:** that which separates us from God "Jehovah" is the title given to the God of the Old Testament—the premortal Jesus Christ.
D&C 110:4–6	• Tell six things that the Lord said to Joseph and Oliver. (vv. 4–5) • Why did the Lord tell the people to rejoice? (vv. 5–6)	**advocate:** a person who pleads in behalf of another
D&C 110:7–8	• During the dedicatory prayer, Joseph prayed that the Lord would accept the temple (D&C 109:78). Why do you think it was important for Joseph to know that the Lord accepted the temple? (v. 7) • What did the Lord say He would do, and what did He expect the Saints to do? (v. 8) • In what ways might someone pollute the temple?	**pollute:** to make something impure

<table>
<tr><th>VERSES</th><th>SUGGESTED QUESTIONS</th><th>TREASURES OF KNOWLEDGE</th></tr>
<tr><td>D&C 110:11–12</td><td>• Who appeared next to Joseph and Oliver, and what keys did he give them? (v. 11)
• Who appeared after Moses and what keys did he give them? (v. 12)

* Bruce R. McConkie, Mormon Doctrine (Salt Lake City: Bookcraft, 1979), 220.
** Stephen E. Robinson and H. Dean Garrett, A Commentary on the Doctrine and Covenants (Salt Lake City: Deseret Book, 2000), 4:66.
*** Ibid., 4:66.
**** Teachings of Presidents of the Church: Joseph Smith (Salt Lake City: The Church of Jesus Christ of Latter-day Saints, 2007), 472.</td><td>keys: spiritual authority
dispensation: “a period of time in which the Lord has at least one authorized servant on the earth who bears the holy priesthood and the keys, and who has a divine commission to dispense the gospel to the inhabitants of the earth” (Bible Dictionary, “Dispensations,” 657).

“We have no information, at this time, as to the mortal life or ministry of Elias. Apparently he lived in the days of Abraham.”*

“There is no separate ‘gospel of Abraham.’ ”** Joseph and Oliver were given the “keys of the gospel as Abraham lived it.… Specifically, these keys included the power to direct temple ordinances beyond the initiatory ordinances … and also the right to organize eternal families.”***</td></tr>
<tr><td>D&C 110:13–16</td><td>• Who appeared to Joseph and Oliver in the next vision? (v. 13)
• The prophet Elijah will come before what event? (v. 14)
• What was Elijah sent to do? (v. 15)
• What keys did Elijah give? (v. 16)</td><td>Elijah was the last Old Testament prophet to hold the sealing powers.

Joseph Smith taught that “the word turn here should be translated bind, or seal.”****</td></tr>
</table>

LESSON TWENTY-TWO

Enduring Trials—Joseph Smith in Prison

BACKGROUND

In the summer of 1836 the Saints that were living in Clay County, Missouri, were asked to leave. The Saints moved sixty miles north and established the town of Far West, Missouri. Between 1836 and 1838 the Saints lived there in relative peace.

In Kirtland, however, the persecution of the Saints escalated to the point that it was no longer safe for the Prophet and most of the members of the Church. In January 1838, most of them left Kirtland and moved to Far West, Missouri.

By October 1838, things were not going well for Joseph or the Saints. Persecution, anger, and violence increased. The residents of Missouri, along with angry members who had left the Church, began to spread lies about Joseph and the Church. Once again the people of Missouri began to fear the Mormons.

On October 27, 1838, Governor Boggs of Missouri issued an extermination order against the Saints, meaning that if they didn't leave the state, the Mormons would be killed.

WORD QUEST
- pavilion
- oppressions
- bowels
- adversity
- endure
- foes
- hail
- derision
- perils
- billowing surge
- hedge

On October 31, 1838, Joseph Smith and fifty other leaders were arrested (all but six were later released), and were imprisoned in Liberty Jail until April 1839.

While Joseph was in prison, more than twelve thousand Saints were once again forced out of their homes; many were robbed, beaten, and killed. They were left "to wander as exiles on the earth… Many sickened and died in consequence of the cold and hardships they had to endure."* The exiled Saints left the state of Missouri and found safety and shelter in the state of Illinois.

In March 1839, while in prison, Joseph prayed to the Lord for help, and received revelations that are now D&C 121–123.

VERSES	SUGGESTED QUESTIONS	TREASURES OF KNOWLEDGE
D&C 121:1–3, 6	• Name four questions that Joseph asked God. (vv. 1–3) • How do you think Joseph was feeling at this time?	**pavilion:** a covering **oppressions:** burdens placed on people by those in authority **bowels:** feelings of compassion

* Joseph Smith. *History of The Church of Jesus Christ of Latter-day Saints.* Edited by B. H. Roberts. 2d ed. rev. 7 vols. (Salt Lake City: The Church of Jesus Christ of Latter-day Saints, 1932–51), 4:539–40.

Note: The remaining verses are God's answer to Joseph's prayer.

VERSES	SUGGESTED QUESTIONS	TREASURES OF KNOWLEDGE
D&C 121:7–8	• What counsel does God give to Joseph? (vv. 7–8) • How long did God say Joseph's adversities and afflictions would last? (v. 7) • What do you think it means to endure "well"? • What kind of attitude should we have through our trials? • If Joseph endures his trials well, how will he be blessed? (v. 8)	**adversity:** trials or hardship **endure:** to be obedient to our covenants with God throughout our lives **foes:** enemies
D&C 121:9–10	• How did Joseph's friends treat him? (v. 9) • Who does God compare Joseph to? (v. 10) • How did Job's friends treat him? (v. 10)	**hail:** welcome Job is a man in the Old Testament who suffered many trials in his life but still remained faithful to God. Job's friends told him the reason he was having so many trials was because he must have committed some great sin (see Job 4, especially vv. 6–8). After his trials were over, Job was given great blessings from God because of his faith and patience.
D&C 122:1–3	• Name five prophesies the Lord gives to Joseph concerning his future. (vv. 1–3)	**derision:** to mock or laugh at

VERSES	SUGGESTED QUESTIONS	TREASURES OF KNOWLEDGE
D&C 122:5–6	• Name three perils Joseph was called to go through. (v. 5) • When Joseph went to Liberty Jail, his family was saddened and afraid for his life. Describe what Joseph's son said before he left. (v. 6) • How do you think Joseph's family felt when he was taken away?	**perils:** danger Joseph Smith stated that before the Church leaders were taken to jail they were allowed to see their families. "I found my wife and children in tears…. My partner wept, my children clung to me, until they were thrust by the swords of the guards."*
D&C 122:7	• Name seven experiences that Joseph may have to endure. (v. 7) • What does the Lord say these trials will give Joseph? (v. 7) • How do you think trials can be for our good?	**billowing surge:** large waves **hedge:** to block or stop
D&C 122:8–9	• Who has suffered more trials than anyone else? (v. 8) • What counsel does the Lord give Joseph? (v. 9) • Why should Joseph not fear? (v. 9) • What does Joseph's experience teach you about enduring trials?	"The Son of Man descended below them all": This refers to the Atonement of Jesus Christ, when He suffered all the pains of mankind, "Which suffering caused myself, even God, the greatest of all, to tremble because of pain, and to bleed at every pore" (D&C 19:18). "Art thou greater than He?" If Jesus Christ, who is perfect, experienced the greatest of all suffering, then we, as imperfect mortals, should never feel that our suffering is unfair or too hard for us to bear.

* Joseph Smith. *History of The Church of Jesus Christ of Latter-day Saints*. Edited by B. H. Roberts. 2d ed. rev. 7 vols. (Salt Lake City: The Church of Jesus Christ of Latter-day Saints, 1932–51), 3:193.

LESSON TWENTY-THREE

Temple Ordinances Restored

BACKGROUND

In the winter of 1838 and 1839, the Saints who were forced out of Missouri found refuge in the city of Quincy, Illinois. The local citizens were kind and sympathetic to the Mormons and gave them much needed help. Because of the great number of people (almost ten thousand) living in Quincy and the surrounding areas, Church leaders bought land in Commerce, Illinois, along the Mississippi river. The city name was later changed to Nauvoo, which "is of Hebrew origin, and signifies a beautiful situation, or place."*

Nauvoo soon became one of the largest cities in Illinois. The Saints lived happy and productive lives there for over six years.

Construction on the Nauvoo temple began in February 1841. By November 1841 the baptismal font was completed and baptisms for the dead were performed. Previous to that, baptisms for the dead were performed in the Mississippi River.

The Nauvoo Temple was completed and dedicated in April 1846, but was destroyed by mobs in November 1848 after the Saints had left to go west. Under the direction of President Gordon B. Hinckley, the Nauvoo Temple was rebuilt and dedicated in June 2002.

WORD QUEST
- ordinance
- deign
- similitude

GOSPEL ART PICTURE KIT

501

* Joseph Smith. *History of The Church of Jesus Christ of Latter-day Saints.* Edited by B. H. Roberts. 2d ed. rev. 7 vols. (Salt Lake City: The Church of Jesus Christ of Latter-day Saints, 1932–51), 4:268.

PART I—BAPTISM FOR THE DEAD

VERSES	SUGGESTED QUESTIONS	TREASURES OF KNOWLEDGE
D&C 124:26–27	• What is the Lord telling the Saints to do and why does He want them to do it?	"Most High" is a reference to both God the Father and His Son, Jesus Christ.
D&C 124:28–29	• What does the Lord want to restore? (v. 29) • Why does the Lord want a baptismal font built in the temple? (v. 29)	
D&C 124:40–41	• In whose name was the temple to be built? (v. 40) • What did the Lord want to reveal? (v. 41)	**ordinance:** a religious act. According to Elder John A. Widtsoe, an early Church apostle, "An ordinance is an earthly symbol of a spiritual reality. It is usually also an act symbolizing a covenant or agreement with the Lord … an act that connects heaven and earth."* **deign:** to condescend (stoop low) to give The dispensation of "the fulness of times is the final dispensation, and began with the revelation of the gospel to Joseph Smith.… There are also things reserved for the fulness of times that have not been revealed previously" (Bible Dictionary, "Dispensations," 657).

* Hoyt W. Brewster Jr., *Doctrine and Covenants Encyclopedia* (Salt Lake City: Deseret Book, 1988), 404.

VERSES	SUGGESTED QUESTIONS	TREASURES OF KNOWLEDGE
D&C 127:5, 7	• Does an earthly ordinance stay with us when we die? (v. 7) • What does verse 7 teach us about the importance of temple work?	
D&C 128:12, 13	• Baptism is likened to what? (v. 12) • The baptismal font is a similitude of what? (v. 13) • Why is the baptismal font in the basement of the temple? (v. 13)	**similitude:** likeness or comparison

PART II—TEMPLE MARRIAGE

VERSES	SUGGESTED QUESTIONS	TREASURES OF KNOWLEDGE
D&C 131:1–4	• How many degrees are in the celestial kingdom? (v. 1) • How does someone obtain the highest degree? (v. 2) • What if someone is not married in the temple? (vv. 3–4) • What do these verses teach you about the importance of temple marriage? • Why do you think temple work is so important for those who have died without going to the temple? • What goals can you make in your life to help those spirits who need their temple work done?	

LESSON TWENTY-FOUR

Discerning Spirits

BACKGROUND

Many of the early Saints were privileged to receive visits from angels and heavenly beings. However, sometimes these visions were not from God, but from Satan, attempting to deceive and lead the Saints away from the Church. The teachings contained in D&C 129 are valuable for all who seek to know the true teachings of God.

This revelation is dated February 1843, while the Saints were in Nauvoo. However, some reports show that these teachings were known by Joseph Smith and others earlier.

WORD QUEST
- just

VERSES	SUGGESTED QUESTIONS	TREASURES OF KNOWLEDGE
D&C 129:1–3	• What two types of heavenly beings are there? (vv. 1–3) • What does a resurrected body have? (v. 1)	**just:** righteous "Spirits of just men made perfect": The spirits of righteous persons who have died, but have not been resurrected.
D&C 129:4–7	• What should you do if a heavenly messenger visits you? (v. 4) • What will he do if he is an angel? (v. 5) • What will the "spirit of a just man made perfect" do? (v. 7)	"An angel of God never has wings."*
D&C 129:8–9	• If the messenger is a devil disguised as an angel of light, what will he do when you ask to shake his hand? (v. 8) • How will you know if he is a devil? (v. 8) • Review the three ways to know if an angel is from God or the devil. • Why do you think this information is important to know?	

* Joseph Smith. *History of The Church of Jesus Christ of Latter-day Saints.* Edited by B. H. Roberts. 2d ed. rev. 7 vols. (Salt Lake City: The Church of Jesus Christ of Latter-day Saints, 1932–51), 3:392.

LESSON TWENTY-FIVE

Where Is Heaven? and Other Gospel Truths

BACKGROUND

On Sunday, April 2, 1843, the Prophet Joseph was visiting a group of Saints in Ramus, Illinois, where Elder Orson Hyde, a member of the Twelve, spoke to the congregation. After the meeting, while eating dinner with his sister Sophronia, the Prophet "told Elder Hyde that [he] was going to offer some corrections to his sermon this morning. [Elder Hyde] replied, 'They shall be thankfully received.' "*

Joseph then preached to the Saints several different gospel truths that are now found in D&C 130.

WORD QUEST

- reckoning
- minister
- prophesy
- suffice
- diligence
- predicated
- tarry

* Joseph Smith. *History of The Church of Jesus Christ of Latter-day Saints.* Edited by B. H. Roberts. 2d ed. rev. 7 vols. (Salt Lake City: The Church of Jesus Christ of Latter-day Saints, 1932–51), 5:323.

VERSES	SUGGESTED QUESTIONS	TREASURES OF KNOWLEDGE
D&C 130:1–2	• What does the Savior look like? (v. 1) • What will our sociality (life) be like in the spirit world? (v. 2)	
D&C 130:4–5	• The reckoning of time is according to what? (v. 4) • Who are the angels who minister to us here on earth? (v. 5)	**reckoning:** the act of counting **minister:** to serve
D&C 130:6–7	• Describe where angels reside. (v. 7)	
D&C 130:8–9	• The place where God resides is what? (v. 8) • What will the earth be like in its sanctified and immortal state? (v. 9) • The earth will be whose? (v. 9)	Urim and Thummim "means Lights and Perfections. An instrument prepared of God to assist man in obtaining revelation from the Lord and in translating languages.… This earth in its celestial condition will be a Urim and Thummim, and many within that kingdom will have an additional Urim and Thummim" (Bible Dictionary, "Urim and Thummim," 787). "Sanctified and immortal state": After the Millennium the earth will change and obtain a celestial glory where celestial beings will dwell.

VERSES	SUGGESTED QUESTIONS	TREASURES OF KNOWLEDGE
D&C 130:12–13	• What future event in the United States did Joseph prophesy about? (vv. 12–13) • Why did Joseph receive this prophesy? (v. 13)	**prophesy:** to declare by divine inspiration something that will happen in the future. Joseph's prophesy about the U.S. Civil War came true. The war did begin over the issue of slavery and began in South Carolina in April 1861—eighteen years after Joseph's prophesy.
D&C 130:14–17	• What did Joseph pray to know about? (v. 14) • What was the Lord's answer? (v. 15) • What was Joseph's interpretation of his answer? (vv. 16–17)	**suffice:** be enough When the Savior was on the earth, He told his disciples of His Second Coming: "Of that day and hour knoweth no man, no, not the angels of heaven, but my Father only" (Matthew 24:36).
D&C 130:18–19	• Do we take our intelligence (knowledge of what we've learned) with us when we die? (v. 18) • Why do we want to obtain knowledge during our lifetime? (v. 19)	**diligence:** constant effort

VERSES	SUGGESTED QUESTIONS	TREASURES OF KNOWLEDGE
D&C 130:20–21	• Explain the law on how we obtain blessings from God. (v. 21) • How does understanding this law affect how you feel about keeping the commandments?	**predicated:** based or established "Irrevocably decreed": a command from God that is impossible to change. All blessings that we receive from keeping the commandments were decided before we came to earth. God is fair; when we keep His commandments we are blessed. When we don't, we miss out on those blessings.
D&C 130:22–23	• What are Heavenly Father and Jesus' bodies like? (v. 22) • What does the Holy Ghost not have and why? (v. 22)	**tarry:** to remain with

LESSON TWENTY-SIX

Articles of Faith

BACKGROUND

In the spring of 1842, while living in Nauvoo, Joseph Smith was asked by John Wentworth, a newspaper editor in Chicago, Illinois, to send him information about The Church of Jesus Christ of Latter–day Saints. Joseph responded by writing a short history of the Church, along with thirteen statements about the Church's beliefs. These statements, known as the Articles of Faith, are considered scripture and can be found at the end of the Pearl of Great Price.

GOSPEL ART PICTURE KIT

618

WORD QUEST

- principle
- repentance
- immersion
- evangelists
- dictates
- conscience
- subject
- magistrates
- benevolent
- admonition

VERSES	SUGGESTED QUESTIONS	TREASURES OF KNOWLEDGE
Article of Faith 1	• Who do we believe in? • Do we believe they are all separate Beings?	
Article of Faith 2	• What will men be punished for? • What will men not be punished for?	Transgression and sin are often used synonymously to identify breaking a law or commandment. However, Adam and Eve did not sin when they partook of the fruit because they did not know right from wrong or good from evil; they had not yet eaten the fruit from the tree of knowledge of good and evil. To sin, one must do "the opposite of what he knows is right."* When Adam and Eve partook of the fruit in the Garden of Eden, they transgressed the law of God and became the first mortals on the earth. Some churches believe that everyone is born a sinner because of the transgression of Adam and Eve. The second Article of Faith states that we believe each person is held accountable for only his own sins.

* Orson F. Whitney, as quoted in Bruce R. McConkie, *Mormon Doctrine* (Salt Lake City: Bookcraft, 1979), 735.

VERSES	SUGGESTED QUESTIONS	TREASURES OF KNOWLEDGE
Article of Faith 3	• How are we saved?	"Ordinances of the gospel" are such things as baptism, receiving the Holy Ghost, and temple marriage. To be saved in the celestial kingdom, we need to receive these ordinances and follow God's commandments the best we can. The Atonement of Jesus Christ makes up for our weaknesses and allows us to live with Him and be like Him one day.
Article of Faith 4	• What are the four principles and ordinances of the gospel? • Why do you think faith in Jesus Christ is the first principle? • Why do you think it's important to repent?	**principle:** beliefs or truths that influence our actions **repentance:** to change **immersion:** when the whole body is covered by water Faith is not just the belief in something; it is also acting on that belief. When we have faith in Jesus Christ, we have a desire to follow Him and be like Him. To properly repent, we need to recognize what we're doing wrong, have a desire to change, and be willing to do whatever it takes to make the change.

VERSES	SUGGESTED QUESTIONS	TREASURES OF KNOWLEDGE
Article of Faith 5	• By what manner is a man called to preach and administer the gospel? • Why do you think it's important to know that the prophet, apostles, bishops, and so forth are called of God?	
Article of Faith 6	• Why do you think it's important to know that we have the same organization in the Church today that existed during Jesus' mortal ministry?	**evangelists:** patriarchs "The Primitive Church" is the church that Jesus Christ established during His mortal life.
Article of Faith 7	• Name five gifts that we believe are given to us. • Talk about the benefit of having each gift.	
Article of Faith 8	• What books of scripture do we believe in? • What do we believe is the difference between the Bible and the Book of Mormon?	The Bible was written by inspired men over the course of thousands of years. We believe that when it was first written, it contained the word of God to man. However, because of the many different translations and changes made by men over the years, we also believe that there are errors, and that "many parts which are plain and most precious" (1 Nephi 13:26) were taken out. "Let the Bible then be read reverently and with prayerful care, the reader ever seeking the light of the Spirit that he may discern between truth and the errors of men."*

* James E. Talmage, *A Study of the Articles of Faith* (Salt Lake City: The Church of Jesus Christ of Latter-day Saints, 1947), 237.

VERSES	SUGGESTED QUESTIONS	TREASURES OF KNOWLEDGE
Article of Faith 9	• What do we believe about revelations from God? • Why is this important for you to know?	
Article of Faith 10	• Name four things we believe in. • Where will Zion be built? • What will happen to the earth after the millennium?	"Gathering of Israel": Jacob (from the Old Testament; his name was later changed to Israel by the Lord) had twelve sons whose descendents made up the kingdom of Israel. Each of Israel's sons had a tribe named after them. Ten of the tribes were captured by the Assyrians and scattered among other nations. This is why they are called "the lost ten tribes of Israel." No one knows who or where they are, but one day they will return to live in Zion. Zion, the New Jerusalem, is where Christ and His followers will live according to celestial laws during the Millennium. "Paradisiacal glory" of the earth: Currently the earth is in a telestial state of glory. During the Millennium, the physical characteristics of the earth will change to that of a terrestrial glory. After the Millennium, the earth will receive a celestial glory, where celestial beings will reside.

VERSES	SUGGESTED QUESTIONS	TREASURES OF KNOWLEDGE
Article of Faith 11	• What privilege do we claim? • Do we believe that everyone has to believe the same as we do? • How should we treat others who believe differently?	**dictates:** a guiding principle **conscience:** the light of Christ that is in everyone; an inner sense of right and wrong
Article of Faith 12	• We believe in being subject to who and what? • What does this teach you about the importance of obeying the laws of the land?	**subject:** to live under the rule or authority of a governing power **magistrates:** judges
Article of Faith 13	• Name ten characteristics we believe in having. • What do we seek after? • Why is each of these characteristics important to have?	**benevolent:** a desire to help others **admonition:** counsel or advice Paul lived after Jesus had died in Jerusalem. He was first a Jew and did not believe in Jesus, but was later converted after he saw a vision of the resurrected Jesus. He became a great apostle of Jesus Christ and taught the gospel in many nations. His teachings can be found in the New Testament.

LESSON TWENTY-SEVEN

Martyrdom of the Prophet

BACKGROUND

The Saints lived in relative peace in the city of Nauvoo for several years. However, problems within the Church and from surrounding neighbors soon began to arise. Several prominent Church leaders were excommunicated and became bitter enemies of Joseph Smith; they spread lies and stirred up anger among the non-Mormons around them.

In 1844 several hundred citizens who opposed Joseph Smith and his teachings started a newspaper called *The Nauvoo Expositor,* which printed negative, untrue articles about Joseph and the Church. The Nauvoo city council, which Joseph was a part of, voted to have the printing press of the newspaper destroyed because they feared the paper would further anger the enemies of the Church and cause violence and persecution to Church members.

The owners of the printing press were angry and pressed charges against the Nauvoo city council. The Governor of Illinois promised Joseph that if he came to Carthage, Illinois, to answer to the charges, he would be protected. Joseph did not think he would be safe, and felt instead that he and his brother Hyrum should leave and go west to prepare a place for the Saints. On June

WORD QUEST
- martyrdom

22, 1844, Joseph and Hyrum crossed the river to head west; however they were encouraged by some to return to Nauvoo because the Saints feared they would be attacked if Joseph left.

Joseph and Hyrum surrendered themselves and went to Carthage, Illinois, where Joseph knew he would be killed. He said "I am going like a lamb to the slaughter; but I am calm as a summer's morning; I have a conscience void of offense towards God, and towards all men. I shall die innocent, and it shall yet be said of me—he was murdered in cold blood" (D&C 135:4).

On June 27, 1844, Joseph and Hyrum Smith were both killed by a mob of over one hundred men who broke into the jail and shot them. Also in the jail that day were two members of the Twelve Apostles: John Taylor and Willard Richards. John Taylor was wounded, and Willard Richards was unharmed during the shootings.

SUGGESTED QUESTIONS

- What did the Nauvoo council vote to do that caused Joseph and Hyrum to have to go to jail?
- What did the Governor of Illinois promise Joseph? Did Joseph believe him?
- What did Joseph feel he and Hyrum should do?
- Why did Joseph and Hyrum surrender and go to Carthage?
- Did Joseph know he was going to die? How do you think he might have felt?

VERSES	SUGGESTED QUESTIONS	TREASURES OF KNOWLEDGE
D&C 135:1	• Why did John Taylor write this document? • Where and when were Joseph and Hyrum shot? • Describe what happened when Joseph and Hyrum were shot.	**martyrdom:** the death of a martyr

VERSES	SUGGESTED QUESTIONS	TREASURES OF KNOWLEDGE
D&C 135:2	• Who else was in the room with Hyrum and Joseph? • What happened to John Taylor? • What happened to Willard Richards?	
D&C 135:3	• Name five things that Joseph Smith did for the salvation of men in this world. • Why do you think each of these is important for our salvation? • Have each family member name at least one thing they are grateful to Joseph Smith for. • A martyr is someone who would rather die than deny their beliefs. What does the death of Joseph Smith teach you about standing up for what you believe in? • Why do you think it's important to have a testimony that Joseph Smith is a prophet of God? • Challenge each family member to pray and ask for a testimony that Joseph Smith is a true prophet.	

LESSON TWENTY-EIGHT

Brigham Young Leads the Church

GOSPEL ART PICTURE KIT

507

STORY

After the death of the Prophet Joseph Smith on June 27, 1844, the members were confused as to who would lead the Church. Joseph was the first prophet of the modern-day Church and the Lord had not yet revealed how a new prophet would be chosen.

However, before Joseph had died, he gave the keys of the priesthood and the apostleship to the members of the Quorum of the Twelve Apostles. According to Brigham Young, "Joseph said to the Twelve, 'I have laid the foundation and you must build thereon, for upon your shoulders the kingdom rests.' "*

Nevertheless, Sidney Rigdon, who was Joseph's first counselor in the First Presidency, felt that he should lead the Church. Sidney stated that he had received a vision that he was to continue to be a spokesman for Joseph, and that he should be the guardian of the Church.

* Joseph Smith. *History of The Church of Jesus Christ of Latter-day Saints*. Edited by B. H. Roberts. 2d ed. rev. 7 vols. (Salt Lake City: The Church of Jesus Christ of Latter-day Saints, 1932–51), 7:230.

In August 1844 a special meeting was held to choose a guardian or president of the Church. Sidney Rigdon first spoke to the congregation for an hour and a half, but was unable to convince the Saints that he was speaking the will of God.

Brigham Young addressed the Saints afterward and told them that the keys of the kingdom were with the Twelve Apostles, and if they wanted to follow God, they should follow the Twelve. Many people present at the meeting witnessed a miracle. They reported that as Brigham spoke, he was transfigured—he looked and sounded like Joseph Smith. "It seemed in the eyes of the people as though it was the very person of Joseph which stood before them."*

One man attending the meeting stated that as soon as he heard Brigham Young speak he "jumped upon [his] feet, for in every possible degree it was Joseph's voice, and his person, in look, attitude, dress and appearance was Joseph himself, personified; and [he] knew in a moment the spirit and mantle of Joseph was upon him.' "**

This miraculous event was a testimony to the Saints, who had felt like sheep without a shepherd, as to who God wanted them to follow. After the meeting, Brigham Young asked the congregation who they wanted to lead them: Sidney Rigdon or the Twelve. Every person present voted to sustain the Twelve Apostles as the leaders of the Church.

From that time forward, Brigham Young led the Church as the President of the Twelve. In December 1847, after arriving in the Salt Lake Valley, he was officially set apart as prophet, seer, and revelator of the Church.

SUGGESTED QUESTIONS

- Why were the Saints confused as to who would be the next prophet?
- What man thought he should be the guardian of the Church, and why did he think this?
- Who did Joseph Smith give the keys and authority to lead the Church to, and why is that important to know?
- What two men spoke at the special meeting to choose a new president?
- What happened when Brigham Young spoke at the meeting?
- Why do you think the Lord allowed the Saints to witness such a miraculous event?
- Who did the Saints choose to lead the Church?
- When did Brigham Young become the prophet?
- How is the next prophet chosen in our day? Why do you think the Lord has established a pattern for choosing prophets?
- Who is the prophet of our Church today, and do you sustain (support and follow) him as the leader of our Church?

* *Church History in the Fulness of Times* (Salt Lake City: The Church of Jesus Christ of Latter-day Saints, 2000), 48, 292.

** *Church History in the Fulness of Times* (Salt Lake City: The Church of Jesus Christ of Latter-day Saints, 2000), 48, 291.

LESSON TWENTY-NINE

The Saints Go West

BACKGROUND

After the death of Joseph Smith in June 1844, persecution against the Mormons did not stop, and by November 1845, the Saints were making preparations to leave Nauvoo. As difficult as it was for the Saints to leave their homes, this time they were able to prepare in getting wagons, food, clothing, and supplies, and even sold some of their homes.

In February 1846, the first group of Saints left Nauvoo and traveled three hundred miles to Winter Quarters in Iowa, where they spent the winter months of 1846–47, waiting and preparing for the remainder of their journey. In July 1847, the Saints began to arrive in the Salt Lake Valley where they have been able to live in peace even until today.

On January 14, 1847, while at Winter Quarters, Brigham Young received a revelation from the Lord that gave instructions and commandments for the Saints as they continued their trek to the West.

GOSPEL ART PICTURE KIT

414, 415

WORD QUEST

- statutes
- cease
- edifying
- merry
- supplication
- ignorant
- humble

VERSES	SUGGESTED QUESTIONS	TREASURES OF KNOWLEDGE
D&C 136:1–2	• Who was this revelation given to? (v. 1) • What covenant and promises are the Saints asked to keep? (v. 2)	**statutes:** laws
D&C 136:17, 20–21	• Why should the Saints not fear their enemies? (v. 17) • Name three things the Saints are counseled to do. (vv. 20–21)	"God of Abraham and of Isaac and of Jacob": This phrase is used throughout the scriptures as a reference to Jesus Christ. He who was born in Bethlehem, died on Calvary, and then resurrected three days later is the same God that was worshipped in Old Testament times by the ancient prophets Abraham, Isaac, and Jacob.
D&C 136:23–24	• Name three things the Saints are told to cease doing. • In what way should we speak to one another? (v. 24)	**cease:** stop **edifying:** to morally or spiritually uplift

VERSES	SUGGESTED QUESTIONS	TREASURES OF KNOWLEDGE
D&C 136:25–26	• What should we do if we borrow something from someone? (v. 25) • What if we can't pay back something we owe to someone else? (v. 25) • What should we do if we lose something we have borrowed? (v. 26)	
D&C 136:28–30	• How can we show the Lord we are merry? (v. 28) • What should we do when we are sorrowful? (v. 29) • Should we fear our enemies? (v. 30)	**merry:** cheerful **supplication:** humble prayer
D&C 136:31–33	• Why are God's people tried in all things? (v. 31) • How do we learn wisdom? (v. 32) • What is the Spirit sent forth to do? (v. 33)	**ignorant:** lacking in knowledge **humble:** to be teachable, willing to learn "Why is it important for God's people to 'bear chastisement'? The scriptures teach that chastening is a cleansing process, it may lead to forgiveness of sins, it teaches us obedience, and it refines us as pure gold."*

* *Doctrine and Covenants Student Manual* (Salt Lake City: The Church of Jesus Christ of Latter-day Saints, 2001), 238–39.

VERSES	SUGGESTED QUESTIONS	TREASURES OF KNOWLEDGE
D&C 136:34, 36	• What did many people in the nation reject? (v. 34) • What did some who rejected the gospel do? (v. 36) • Who is verse 36 referring to?	
D&C 136:39, 41–42	• Why was the way in which Joseph Smith died considered "needful" by the Lord? (v. 39) • Why should we be diligent in keeping the commandments? (v. 42)	"Prophets do not give their lives casually… The death of Joseph and Hyrum Smith is undisputable evidence of the truthfulness of the gospel of Jesus Christ, restored in these latter days."*

* Stephen E. Robinson and H. Dean Garrett, *A Commentary on the Doctrine and Covenants* (Salt Lake City: Deseret Book, 2000), 4:293.

LESSON THIRTY

The Savior's Visit to the Spirit World

BACKGROUND

Joseph F. Smith was the son of Hyrum Smith and nephew to Joseph Smith. He was born in 1838 while his father was in jail in Missouri. Joseph F. Smith was seven years old when his mother, Mary Fielding Smith, took her family and left Nauvoo to go west with the Saints. She died when he was only thirteen years old. When Joseph was twenty-eight he became a member of the Quorum of the Twelve Apostles, and in 1901 he became the sixth president of the Church.

President Smith received the vision recorded in D&C 138 on October 3, 1918. The next day during general conference, "President Smith declared that he had received several divine communications during the previous months. One of these, concerning the Savior's visit to the spirits of the dead while his body was in the tomb, he had received the previous day. It was written immediately following the close of the conference; on October 31, 1918, it was submitted to the counselors in the First Presidency, the Council of the Twelve, and the Patriarch, and it was unanimously accepted by them" (D&C 138 heading).

President Smith died just a few weeks after receiving this remarkable vision.

WORD QUEST

- innumerable
- ungodly
- defiled
- commissioned
- sojourn
- bondage
- immortality
- eternal life

GOSPEL ART PICTURE KIT

412, 511

VERSES	SUGGESTED QUESTIONS	TREASURES OF KNOWLEDGE
D&C 138:12, 15	• What spirits did President Smith see gathered together? (v. 12) • What were the spirits' feelings and why? (v. 15)	**innumerable:** too many to count "The day of their deliverance": these spirits were waiting to be resurrected, to be reunited with their bodies. This would allow them to continue their eternal progression.
D&C 138:18–19	• Who appeared to the multitude of spirits? (v. 18) • What did He preach to them? (v. 19)	
D&C 138:20–22	• Who did the Savior not visit? (vv. 20–21) • What was it like where the wicked were? (v. 22) • What was it like where the righteous were? (v. 22)	**ungodly:** someone who does not believe in God **defiled:** to make unclean or unworthy
D&C 138:28–30	• What did President Smith wonder about? (v. 28) • The Lord organized his forces to do what? (v. 30)	**commissioned:** given power and authority to carry out a particular duty "My eyes were opened and my understanding quickened": By the power of the Holy Ghost we can be shown and taught things that we did not understand before.

VERSES	SUGGESTED QUESTIONS	TREASURES OF KNOWLEDGE
D&C 138:36–37	• How did the Savior spend His days in the spirit world? (v. 36) • Who could the Savior not go to personally? (v. 37)	**sojourn:** a temporary stay To "redeem" means to regain possession of someone who is in captivity. When we sin, we are under Satan's power and control. Through the Atonement, Christ became our Redeemer; He can save us from Satan and the effects of death, so that we are free from the consequences of our sins and can live forever. (See Mosiah 16:3–5, 7–8).
D&C 138:38–47, 49	• Read through the verses and identify ten mighty spirits who were assembled in this vast congregation of the righteous. • Choose five people from the list above and tell one great thing that they did in their lives.	
D&C 138:50–51	• What do the dead consider to be bondage? (v. 50) • What power did the Lord give the righteous? (v. 51)	**bondage:** being held back. Our spirits are limited in what they can do without a body. We will not be perfected until after the resurrection, when our bodies and spirits are reunited forever. **immortality:** the body and spirit together forever, never to separate again. Everyone will receive the gift of immortality after the resurrection. **eternal life:** life with God and life like God; the gift of eternal life is conditioned on one's righteousness.

VERSES	SUGGESTED QUESTIONS	TREASURES OF KNOWLEDGE
D&C 138:53–55	• Name five other people that President Smith saw in his vision. (v. 53) • What were these great men reserved to do? (vv. 53–54) • President Smith said that these men were also among whom? (v. 55)	President Smith is also shown a vision of the leaders from the latter-days, and of their mission in the spirit world.
D&C 138:56–57	• What did many righteous spirits receive before they were born? (v. 56) • What do the faithful elders of this dispensation do when they die? (v. 57)	
D&C 138:58–59	• What will happen to the dead who repent? (vv. 58–59) • What does President Smith bear record of? (v. 60)	"Bear record": to give a witness, in writing, that something is true

Appendix

CHURCH HISTORY TIMELINE

MAP OF CHURCH HISTORY CITIES

WHO'S WHO IN THE DOCTRINE AND COVENANTS

WORD QUEST GLOSSARY

GAMES, GAMES, GAMES!

SCRIPTURE STRIPS

Church History Timeline

1805 Joseph Smith is born

1820 The First Vision

1823 Angel Moroni first visits Joseph Smith

1827 Joseph Smith marries Emma Hale

Joseph Smith receives the gold plates

1830 The Church of Jesus Christ of Latter-day Saints is organized

1831 Saints move to Ohio and Missouri

1833 Saints are forced out of Jackson County, Missouri

1836 Kirtland Temple is dedicated

1838 All Saints gather to Far West, Missouri

Joseph Smith in Liberty Jail

Saints are forced to leave Missouri

1839 City of Nauvoo, Illinois, is established

1842 Relief Society is organized

1844 Joseph and Hyrum Smith are killed

1845 Nauvoo Temple is completed

1846 Saints leave Nauvoo

1847 Saints arrive in Salt Lake Valley

Map of Church History Cities

Who's Who in the Doctrine and Covenants

Do you sometimes forget a person's name that you've studied about? Do you ever read about somebody but can't remember who they were? The following section can help you better know the people in the Doctrine and Covenants stories that are in this guide.

Boggs, Lilburn W.: The Governor of Missouri from 1836–1840; issued the extermination order against the Mormons, which forced thousands of Saints to flee from their homes in Missouri to Illinois.

Cowdery, Oliver: One of the earliest and most well-known members of the Church. He baptized and was baptized by Joseph Smith after John the Baptist restored the Aaronic Priesthood. He was one of the Three Witnesses of the gold plates, was an Assistant to the President of the Church, and was with Joseph when he received other important revelations and visions.

Harris, Lucy: Wife of Martin Harris. Lucy was critical of and questioned Joseph Smith's claim to have the gold plates. She pressured her husband for proof, which resulted in the lost 116 pages of the manuscript. She never joined the Church.

Harris, Martin: Lived in New York by the Smith family and helped Joseph in the translation work of the gold plates. He lost 116 pages of the manuscript, but later repented and was allowed to be one of the Three Witnesses. Martin also provided the funds so that the first copies of the Book of Mormon could be printed.

Hyde, Orson: Joined the Church in 1831, and was baptized by Sidney Rigdon. Orson later became one of the first members of the Quorum of the Twelve Apostles and served faithfully in his calling until his death.

Partridge, Edward: Joined the Church in 1830, just six months after it was organized. In February 1831 he was called to be the first bishop of the Church. He lived in Missouri and suffered afflictions and trials, including being tarred and feathered during a mob attack. He stayed true to the Church until his death.

Phelps, W. W.: William Wines Phelps was in charge of printing the first copies of the Doctrine and Covenants along with printing a newspaper for the Church. His home and printing press were destroyed during a mob attack. William wrote numerous hymns for the Church that are still sung today, including "The Spirit of God" and "Praise to the Man." He died a faithful member of the Church.

Page, Hiram: A member of the Church from the early days in New York. He was one of the Eight Witnesses of the gold plates.

Richards, Willard: A cousin of Brigham Young, who joined the Church in Kirtland in 1836. Willard served as Joseph's secretary and helped write his journals; he later became Church Historian. He became a member of the Quorum of the Twelve Apostles in 1838. Willard was with Joseph, Hyrum, and John Taylor in Carthage jail when Joseph and Hyrum were killed. He was a faithful member of the Church throughout his life.

Rollins, Caroline and Mary Elizabeth: Caroline and her sister Mary are best known for saving pages of the Book of Commandments when a mob attacked the printing press. Caroline and Mary joined the Church in Kirtland, Ohio. They both had strong testimonies of the Book of Mormon and Joseph Smith.

Rigdon, Sidney: A preacher in Ohio, who joined the Church in 1830 and came to New York to assist Joseph Smith. He later became Joseph's first counselor in the First Presidency. He helped Joseph translate the Bible, and was with him when he received numerous revelations. Sidney felt he should be appointed guardian of the Church after Joseph died, but the leadership was given to Brigham Young and the Twelve Apostles. Sidney did not go with the Saints when they went to the Salt Lake Valley.

Smith, Alvin: Oldest son of Lucy Mack and Joseph Smith Sr. Alvin died when he was twenty-five years old, before the Restoration of the Church. Joseph later saw Alvin in a vision, in the celestial kingdom (see D&C 137).

Smith, Catherine: The ninth child of Lucy Mack and Joseph Smith Sr.

Smith, Don Carlos: Joseph's youngest brother, who had a strong testimony of his brother and the restored Church. He was a faithful member during his life and died in Nauvoo at the age of twenty-five.

Smith, Emma Hale: Emma Hale met and married Joseph Smith in 1827. She stood by his side faithfully throughout persecutions and trials. Emma and Joseph had eleven children, two of which were adopted. Six of Emma's babies died when they were born or while still young. Emma was the first Relief Society president and also compiled the first hymnbook. Emma stayed in Nauvoo with her mother-in-law, Lucy, after Joseph was killed and the Saints left to go West. Emma later remarried and died in 1879 when she was seventy-four years old.

Smith, Hyrum: The third child of Lucy Mack and Joseph Smith Sr. Hyrum stood by his brother's side his entire life. He was one of the first six members of the Church when it was organized, and was one of the Eight Witnesses of the gold plates. He served in many callings in the Church, including Church Patriarch. Hyrum's first wife Jerusha died in 1837, leaving him with five children to take care of. Shortly after, he married Mary Fielding and they had two children. Their son, Joseph, later became the sixth president of the Church. Hyrum was killed by a mob while imprisoned in Carthage Jail with his brother Joseph on June 27, 1844.

Smith, Joseph Jr.: The Prophet of the Restoration. Joseph Smith was born in 1805 and received the First Vision when he was only fourteen years old. Joseph Smith translated the Book of Mormon, organized The Church of Jesus Christ of Latter-day Saints, restored the priesthood and temple keys, and helped spread the gospel of Jesus Christ across the earth. Joseph endured many hardships throughout his life, but remained a faithful servant to the Lord. He was killed by a mob on June 27, 1844, while imprisoned in Carthage Jail with his brother Hyrum.

Smith, Joseph Sr.: He was born in 1771. His father, Asel Smith, prophesied that a prophet would be born in his family. Joseph Sr. married Lucy Mack in 1796, and they had eleven children. Joseph Sr. believed in his son Joseph Jr. and was one of his greatest supporters. Joseph Sr. was baptized on April 6, 1830, the day the Church was organized, and was also one of the Eight Witnesses of the gold plates. Joseph Sr. served as the Church Patriarch until his death in 1840.

Smith, Joseph F.: Son of Hyrum and Mary Fielding Smith. He was born in 1838 while his father was in jail in Missouri. Joseph F. Smith was seven years old when his mother, Mary Fielding Smith, took her family and left Nauvoo to come west with the Saints. Joseph's mother died when he was only thirteen years old. When he was twenty-eight years old he became a member of the Twelve Apostles, and in 1901 he became the sixth president of the Church.

Smith, Lucy: The eleventh child of Lucy Mack, and Joseph Smith Sr.

Smith, Lucy Mack: She was born in 1776, and married Joseph Smith Sr. in 1796. Lucy gave birth to eleven children. Lucy was a religious woman who taught her children from the Bible. She believed in and supported her son Joseph in all that he did. Lucy's husband, Joseph Sr., and seven of their children died during her lifetime; three of which died in 1844. Lucy remained faithful to the Church and died in Nauvoo in 1855.

Smith, Mary Fielding: Joined the Church in 1836 while living in Canada with her brother and sister. Mary married Hyrum Smith in 1837 after his wife died. Hyrum and Mary later had two more children, Joseph and Martha. Mary had great faith despite the hardships she had to endure, especially while living in Missouri. Mary and her children came west with the Saints and settled in the Salt Lake Valley. Mary's son, Joseph, became the sixth president of the Church.

Smith, Samuel H.: Sixth child of Lucy Mack and Joseph Smith Sr. He was one of the Eight Witnesses of the gold plates, along with being one of the first six members of the Church. Samuel served faithfully in the Church until his death, just one month after his brothers Joseph and Hyrum were killed.

Smith, Sophronia: Fourth child of Lucy Mack and Joseph Smith Sr.

Smith, William: Eighth child of Lucy Mack and Joseph Smith Sr.

Taylor, John: Joined the Church while living in Canada in 1836. A year later he was called to be a member of the Quorum of the Twelve Apostles. He was with the Prophet, his brother Hyrum, and Willard Richards in Carthage Jail. He was shot by the mob, but later recovered from his wounds. He wrote D&C 135, paying tribute to the great life of Joseph Smith. John Taylor became the third president of the Church.

Whitmer, Christian: One of the Eight Witnesses of the gold plates.

Whitmer, David: One of the Three Witnesses of the gold plates. He was with Oliver Cowdery when the angel Moroni showed them the gold plates. David was also one of the first six members of the Church.

Whitmer, Jacob: One of the Eight Witnesses of the gold plates.

Whitmer, John: One of the Eight Witnesses of the gold plates. John helped serve as Joseph's scribe during the translation of the Book of Mormon and the Bible. He was also called to be Church Historian in the early days of the Church.

Whitmer, Peter Jr.: One of the Eight Witnesses of the gold plates. He served faithfully in the Church until his death in 1836.

Whitmer, Peter Sr.: The Whitmer family offered help and friendship to Joseph while living in New York. Joseph and Emma lived with the Whitmers while translating the Book of Mormon. The Three Witnesses saw the angel Moroni and the gold plates on their property. The Church was first organized at Peter Whitmer's home on April 6, 1830.

Wentworth, John: an editor for a newspaper in Chicago. John wrote to Joseph Smith in 1842, asking for information on the Church. Joseph responded by writing a short history of the Church, along with thirteen statements about the Church's beliefs, which later became known as the Articles of Faith. The letter Joseph sent is often referred to as the Wentworth Letter.

Whitney, Newel K.: Joined the Church while living in Kirtland, Ohio, in 1830. Newel owned a store in Kirtland and allowed Joseph and Emma to live above it after they moved to Ohio from New York. The School of the Prophets, along with other church meetings, were held above his store. In 1831 he was called to be the bishop of the church. He served faithfully in the Church and as a bishop until he died in 1850.

Williams, Fredrick G.: Joined the Church in Kirtland, Ohio, in 1830. He served as Joseph's counselor in the First Presidency while in Kirtland, Ohio. He died in 1842 as a member of the Church.

Young, Brigham: Joined the Church in 1832. Two years later he was called to be a member of the Quorum of the Twelve Apostles. He was a loyal and trusted friend of the Prophet Joseph Smith, and served the Church faithfully during his lifetime. When Joseph died, Brigham, as the president of the Quorum of the Twelve, became the leader of the Church. He was set apart as the second president and prophet of the Church three years later.

Word Quest Glossary

Finding new words and learning their meanings can be exciting and helpful in understanding the scriptures. Keep track of the new words you have discovered by writing down the definitions in your own words; this will help you to remember them better. Often times you will come upon these words again while reading other sections in the Doctrine and Covenants. If you've forgotten their definitions, you can easily look them up here. Enjoy your search!

A

abridgement (p. 15):

abomination (p. 5):

admonition (p. 87):

adultery (p. 40):

adversary (p. 5):

adversity (p. 70):

advocate (p. 66):

aloof (p. 2):

amidst (p. 4):

appendage (p. 58):

ascended (p. 8):

aspire (p. 59):

B

benevolent (p. 87):

billowing surge (p. 71):

bondage (p. 99):

borne (p. 20):

bosom (p. 7):

bowels (p: 69):

broken heart (p. 32):

C

cease (p. 94):

chastened (p. 54)

cleave (p. 35):

commissioned (p. 98):

compulsion (p. 60):

conduit (p. 8):

confound (p. 15):

conscience (p. 87):

consequence (p. 54):

console (p. 34):

constitution (p. 48):

contrite spirit (p. 32):

countenance (p. 7):

creeds (p. 5):

crucified (p. 31):

cunning (p. 14):

D

deceived (p. 37):

defiled (p. 98):

defy (p. 4):

deign (p. 73):

denomination (p. 2):

derision (p. 70):

devilish (p. 31):

dictates (p. 87):

diligence (p. 80):

dispensation (p. 67):

dividing asunder (p. 27):

dominion (p. 60):

E

earnestly (p. 37):

edifying (p. 94):

endure (p. 70):

enlighten (p. 17):

especial (p. 59):

esteemed (p. 54):

eternal life (p. 99):

evangelists (p. 85):

exalts (p. 20):

exerting (p. 4):

exhort (p. 35):

expound (p. 35):

extortion (p. 41):

F

firmament (p. 44):

foes (p. 70):

forbade (p. 5):

forbidden (p. 9):

G

Gentile (p. 30):

grievous (p. 55):

guile (p. 60):

H

hail (p. 70):

hearken (p. 34):

heed (p. 27):

hedge (p. 71):

honorable (p. 44):

humble (p. 95):

hypocrisy (p. 60):

I

ignorant (p. 95):

immersion (p. 84):

immortality (p. 99):

impart (p. 55):

innumerable (p. 98):

J

jarrings (p. 54):

Jew (p. 30):

just (p. 77):

K

keys (p. 67):

kindled (p. 41):

kindreds (p. 7):

L

lest (p. 32):

liberally (p. 4):

M

magistrates (p. 87):

martyrdom (p. 89):

meekness (p. 35):

merry (p. 95):

minister (p. 79):

mourned (p. 54):

murmur (p. 34):

musing (p. 8):

O

oblations (p. 40):

offend (p. 41):

oppressions (p. 69):

ordinance: (p. 73)

P

pavilion (p. 69):

perils (p. 71):

pollute (p. 66):

precepts (p. 55):

poignant (p. 2):

predicated (p. 81):

pride (p. 35):

principle (p. 84):

profited (p. 37):

prophecy (p. 28):

prophesy (p. 80):

proselyte (p. 2):

prudence (p. 48):

R

raiment (p. 41):

reckoning (p. 79):

redemption (p. 55):

remission (p. 32):

repentance (p. 84):

revelation (p. 28):

S

salvation (p. 55):

sanctified (p. 54):

save (p. 17):

saved (p. 31):

scepter (p. 61):

sect (p. 2):

seduced (p. 37):

seer (p. 7):

sensual (p. 31):

similitude (p. 74):

sin (p. 32):

sojourn (p. 99):

sorcerer (p. 45)

statutes (p. 94):

strifes (p. 54):

subject (p. 87):

suffer (p. 14):

suffice (p. 80):

supplication (p. 95):

surpasses (p. 46):

T

tarry (p. 81):

temptation (p. 32):

tongues (p. 7):

transcendent (p. 43):

transgression (p. 31):

trifle (p. 18):

tumult (p. 4):

U

unfeigned (p. 60):

ungodly (p. 98):

upbraideth (p. 4):

upheld (p. 58):

V

valiant (p. 45)

veil (p. 66):

venture (p. 4):

verily (p. 18):

virtue (p. 34):

W

whithersoever (p. 34):

wrath (p. 41):

whoremonger (p. 45)

Z

Zion (p. 17):

Games, Games, Games!

This section contains thirty fun family activities that are quick and easy to prepare. Activities are divided into two sections: activities that help increase knowledge and comprehension of the Doctrine and Covenants, and Just for Fun pioneer games. There are a variety of games to meet the needs of both older and younger children. Enjoy!

ACTIVITIES TO HELP INCREASE COMPREHENSION

Back to the Word

Write different words or draw pictures on pieces of paper and place in a container. (Examples: Joseph Smith, the Kirtland Temple, the angel Moroni, the Book of Mormon, the Word of Wisdom, the Priesthood, Urim and Thummim, Hill Cumorah, the First Vision). One person sits at the front of the room and picks a word. A second person sits with their back to the first person and faces the rest of the family. The person who picked the word holds it up so the family can see the word. The family then yells out clues to try and explain the word to the second person facing them without saying the word. They must guess the given word within a specific time limit. Give each family member a turn to choose a word and to guess a word.

Church History Badminton

Set up a court by placing a rope tied to two chairs. Make two small teams. Give each family member a flyswatter (the racket). Inflate a balloon (this will be the ball). The game is played by hitting the balloon over the string without letting the balloon touch the ground. Each time someone hits the balloon he must call out a person, place, or thing from Church history. If it touches the ground, or if someone can't remember a name, then the opposite team gets a point.

Oops!

Write questions from any lesson on pieces of paper and place in a container. Also add a few cards that say "Oops!" Family members take turns picking a paper, and if they answer the question correctly they get to keep the paper. If they draw an "Oops!" card they must return all their cards (except the "Oops!" card) to the container. The person with the most papers at the end wins.

Musical Cards

Write questions from any lesson on one side of a card, and write a number from 1 to 10 on the other side.

Place all the cards in a circle. Have one family member sit out and be in charge of playing the music and picking numbers. Begin playing the music and have the family walk around the circle of cards. When the music stops have the person sitting out yell a number. If someone is standing on that number, they answer the question on the back. If they get it right they keep the card, but if not, it goes back on the floor. Keep playing until all the cards are gone. The person with the most cards wins.

Hot Potato

Pick a Doctrine and Covenants topic (such as "Who's Who," "Places in Church History," or "Word Quest Words"). Set a timer for a specific amount of time (twenty seconds, one minute, and so forth). Sit in a circle and pass an object around. Each family member must say a word from the chosen topic when they are holding the object. The person holding the object when the timer goes off loses that round.

I Spy

One family member picks a page from the Doctrine and Covenants to read from and says, "I spy with my little eye a word that starts with (says a letter)." The rest of the family has to guess the word. To make it easier, have family members look in their scriptures at the same page.

Word Quest True or False

Put a line of tape on the floor and designate one side "True" and the other "False." Have the family stand on the line and have one person read Word Quest words and definitions from the book. Some of the definitions they give will be true and some false. Each family member decides if the answer is true by jumping on the "True" side of the line or false by jumping on the "False" side. Whoever is wrong sits out until everyone is out but one, who is the winner of that round.

Dress like Dad (or Mom)

Give each family member a shirt, tie, socks and shoes in a bag (if you don't have enough for everyone, play in pairs and take turns). Have someone read a question from the lesson. The first person to answer correctly gets to put on a clothing item from the bag. Keep asking questions until someone is completely dressed. (Optional: Use pioneer clothes and dress like a pioneer.)

Word Quest Tic-tac-toe

Draw a tic-tac-toe board on a piece of paper, and in each square write one Word Quest word. Divide the family into two teams. Each team must pick a word on the paper and give the correct definition before marking an "X" or an "O" over that word. The first team to get three in a row wins.

Whisper Game

Sit in a circle and have one family member begin by whispering a short scripture verse in the person's ear next to them. That person then whispers what he heard in the next person's ear, and so on, until the last family member. The last person then says the verse out loud to see if it's the same as the original verse. For smaller children, say only one or two words to pass along.

Treasure Hunt

(*Note: This game would be best to play after the first twelve lessons have been studied).

Write the following questions/clues on pieces of paper and then hide around the house.

1) What is the name of the hill where Joseph Smith found the gold plates? (answer: The Hill Cumorah) – Go to the front door.

2) What is the name of the angel who gave Joseph Smith the gold plates? (answer: Moroni) – Go to the oldest person's bed.

3) Name the Three Witnesses of the gold plates (answer: Martin Harris, David Whitmer, Oliver Cowdery) – Go to the fridge.

4) Who restored the Aaronic Priesthood to Joseph Smith and Oliver Cowdery? (answer: John the Baptist) – Go to the family room couch.

5) What was Joseph Smith's wife's name? (answer: Emma Hale Smith) – Go to the silverware drawer.

6) What did Joseph use to translate the gold plates? (answer: the Urim and Thummim) – Go to the bathroom sink.

7) On what date was the Church organized? (answer: April 6, 1830) – Go to Mom's (or Dad's) shoes.

8) What is the name of Joseph Smith's father and mother? (answer: Joseph Smith Sr. and Lucy Mack Smith) – Go to the TV (or radio)

9) How old was Joseph Smith when he had the First Vision? (answer: fourteen years old) – Go to the kitchen for treats!

Keep card 1 to start with, and hide the rest of the cards in the following locations: (2) front door, (3) Mom/Dad's bed, (4) fridge, (5) family room couch, (6) silverware drawer, (7) bathroom sink, (8) Mom/Dad's shoes, (9) TV or radio.

To play: Start with card 1, read the question, and if answered correctly read the clue where the next card can be found. Keep playing until the last card is found. The last clue will lead the family to the kitchen for the treat.

Verse Search

Choose a verse from the Doctrine and Covenants and write each word of the verse on a separate piece of paper. Hide each slip of paper around the room or house, and have family members search for the papers. Once all papers are found, work together to put the papers together in the right order. Play again with another verse. Let each family member take turns picking a verse and hiding the papers.

Word Guess

(Play like Hangman.) Have one family member choose a word (a person, place, or thing) and write a dash for each letter of the word on a piece of paper. The other family members take turns guessing a letter. When someone guesses a letter correctly, he rolls the dice to see how many points that letter is worth and gets another turn guessing a letter. The person with the most points when the word is guessed correctly wins. Give each family member a turn at choosing a word to guess.

Question the Answer

Choose two family members to come to the front of the room. Have another person read an answer to a question from the lesson and say, "What's the question?" The fastest player to say the question correctly wins that round. The person who lost sits down and another family members races against the winner.

Clothespin in a Jar

Divide into two teams and give each team a jar and some clothespins (or any small object). One person sits out and reads questions to one team at a time. If the team can answer the question correctly, someone on the team must drop a clothespin into the jar on the first try, standing directly above the jar on the ground. Take turn reading all of the questions to the teams. The team with the most clothespins in its jar at the end wins.

Scripture Scavenger Hunt

Divide the family into teams and give each team a piece of paper with Doctrine and Covenants scripture words written on them. Each team must race to find a scripture reference where that word can be found in the Doctrine and Covenants and write it down. The first team to find all of their references wins. (Possible words to find: Adam-ondi-ahman, Apocrypha, Gentile, Melchizedek Priesthood, Zion, Word of Wisdom, redemption, tithing, heaven, and Hill Cumorah.)

Discern the Truth

Choose one person to ask a question and two (or more) people to answer. The questioner asks a question and the answerers quietly decide together who will give the right answer and who will give an incorrect answer that sounds like the truth. The questioner must discern which answer is correct and which is not. Give each member of the family a turn to play each part.

Who's Who Match

Make enough papers for each member of the family. Write a name from "Who's Who in the Doctrine and Covenants" on one piece of paper and the description on another piece of paper. Pin one paper on the front of each person's shirt. Set a timer for thirty seconds (or fewer) and have the family race to find their matches. When a match is found, have the pair sit down. Whoever is left standing when the timer goes off loses that round.

Taboo

Choose a letter of the alphabet that will be taboo to use in answering questions. Choose one person to be "it." "It" must answer questions given to him from the lesson without using words that contain the taboo letter. As long as he doesn't use the taboo letter he can continue to answer questions. If his answer contains the taboo letter, he is out and another person becomes "it."

Jackstraws

(Play like pickup sticks.) Hold a pile of straws a few inches above the ground with the straws pointing straight up and drop the straws, letting them land in a pile. Each family member takes a turn being asked a question from the lesson. If they answer correctly they can try to remove a straw without moving any other straws in the pile. If successful in doing so, they can keep their straw. Continue asking questions until the straws are gone. The player who has the most straws is the winner. (To make it more challenging, have different colored straws worth extra points.)

PIONEER GAMES—JUST FOR FUN!

Drop the Bandana

(Play like Duck Duck Goose.) Have all but one family member sit in a circle. The person standing out ("it") takes a bandana and walks around the outside of the circle and drops the bandana behind one person sitting down. The person sitting must race to tag "it" before they run around the circle and sit in the empty spot. Keep playing until everyone has had a chance to be "it."

Joseph Smith

(Play like Marco Polo.) One person is blindfolded and the rest of the family scatters around the room or yard. The blindfolded person yells out "Joseph!" and the rest of the family each yells "Smith." The blindfolded person tries to tag one of the family members and they become blindfolded next. Keep playing until everyone has a chance to be blindfolded.

Stick Pull

(Note: This was one of Joseph Smith's favorite activities.) Two family members sit on the floor facing with feet pressed together and knees bent. Each holds onto a smooth stick. On the "go" both players pull on the stick and cannot let go. The first one to pull the other person up is the winner.

Three-legged Race

Pair family members and tie one of each pair's ankles with a rope or bandana. (Make sure the pair is facing the same direction and tie a right leg to a left leg.)
Have a starting line and a finish line. Have all the pair's race to the finish line with the first pair to the end winning.

Sack Race

Give each family member a pillow case to stand inside of. Line everyone up at the starting line, and on the "go" signal have everyone hop in their sack to the finish line. You must stay in your pillowcase the entire race. The first person to the finish line wins.

Linking the Family

Choose one person to be "it." "It" then chases the rest of the family. When "it" tags someone, they must hold hands and together they run to tag someone else. Each time someone is tagged they must hold hands with the chain of "its" until everyone has been tagged.

Poor Doggie

One person is chosen to be "Doggie." The family sits in a circle and Doggie goes to each player and barks, whines, and imitates a dog. The other family members have to pet Doggie and say "Poor Doggie, Poor Doggie." The object of the game is to not smile or laugh while saying this. Whoever smiles becomes the next Doggie.

Who Has the Button?

Have all but one family member sit in a circle. Have one person sit in the middle and be "it." One person in the circle starts out with a button. They begin passing the button around the circle with hands that are cupped and closed. Each person continues doing this around the circle while the person in the middle watches. However, at any time someone can keep the button but pretend to pass it on. If the button does not get passed on, then the other family members continue pretending to pass the button. When the person who started is again passed the button he asks "it": "Button, button, who has the button?" "It" then guesses. If he guesses correctly, he gets to keep the button and can stay in the middle again. If he guesses incorrectly, he goes in the circle and the person who had the button goes in the middle. The person with the most buttons wins.

Tug of War

Divide the family up into two teams, mixing older and younger family members. Use tape to make a line on the floor. Each team stands on either side of the line and holds a rope. On the "go" both teams begin pulling, trying to pull the other team over the line. Whichever team crosses the line loses and must sing their favorite pioneer or primary song. Mix up the teams and play again!

Dumb Crambo

This game is similar to Charades. Have one family member leave the room and the rest of the family decides on a given word, for example, "cat." When the family member returns to the room they are only told a word that rhymes with the given word, such as "bat." The one family member then tries to guess the given word by acting out words that rhyme with "bat," such as "rat," "hat," or "mat." He continues to act out words until someone guesses the given word "cat." Give each family member a turn to guess.

Scripture Strips

Instructions: Cut out the titles below and place in a container. Each time your family gathers for family home evening or scripture study, let someone choose which story or lesson to study by picking a title from the container.

Joseph Smith

The First Vision

The Angel Moroni

The Gold Plates

The Lost Manuscript

Personal Revelation

The Three Witnesses

Witnesses See the Gold Plates

The Priesthood Restored

Serving in the Lord's Kingdom

Organization of the Church

An Elect Lady

Gifts of the Spirit

Blessings of Keeping the Commandments

The Three Degrees of Glory

The Word of Wisdom

Persecution of the Saints in Missouri

Affliction in Zion

The Kirtland Temple

Keys are Restored

Enduring Trials—Joseph Smith in Prison

Priesthood Duties

Temple Ordinances Restored

Discerning Spirits

Where is Heaven?

Articles of Faith

The Martyrdom of a Prophet

Brigham Young Leads the Church

The Saints Go West

The Savior's Visit to the Spirit World

About the Author

Janet Burningham was born and raised in Provo, Utah. After graduating from Brigham Young University with a bachelor's degree in elementary education, she taught school for several years and also developed curriculum for various educational programs. Currently she is a full-time mother.

Janet and her husband, Scott, are the parents of four children: Joshua, Katey, Madeline, and Benjamin.

She enjoys teaching and researching gospel topics, along with reading, walking, enjoying the outdoors, and spending time with family and friends.

You can visit her website at www.janetburningham.com.

0 26575 52064 4